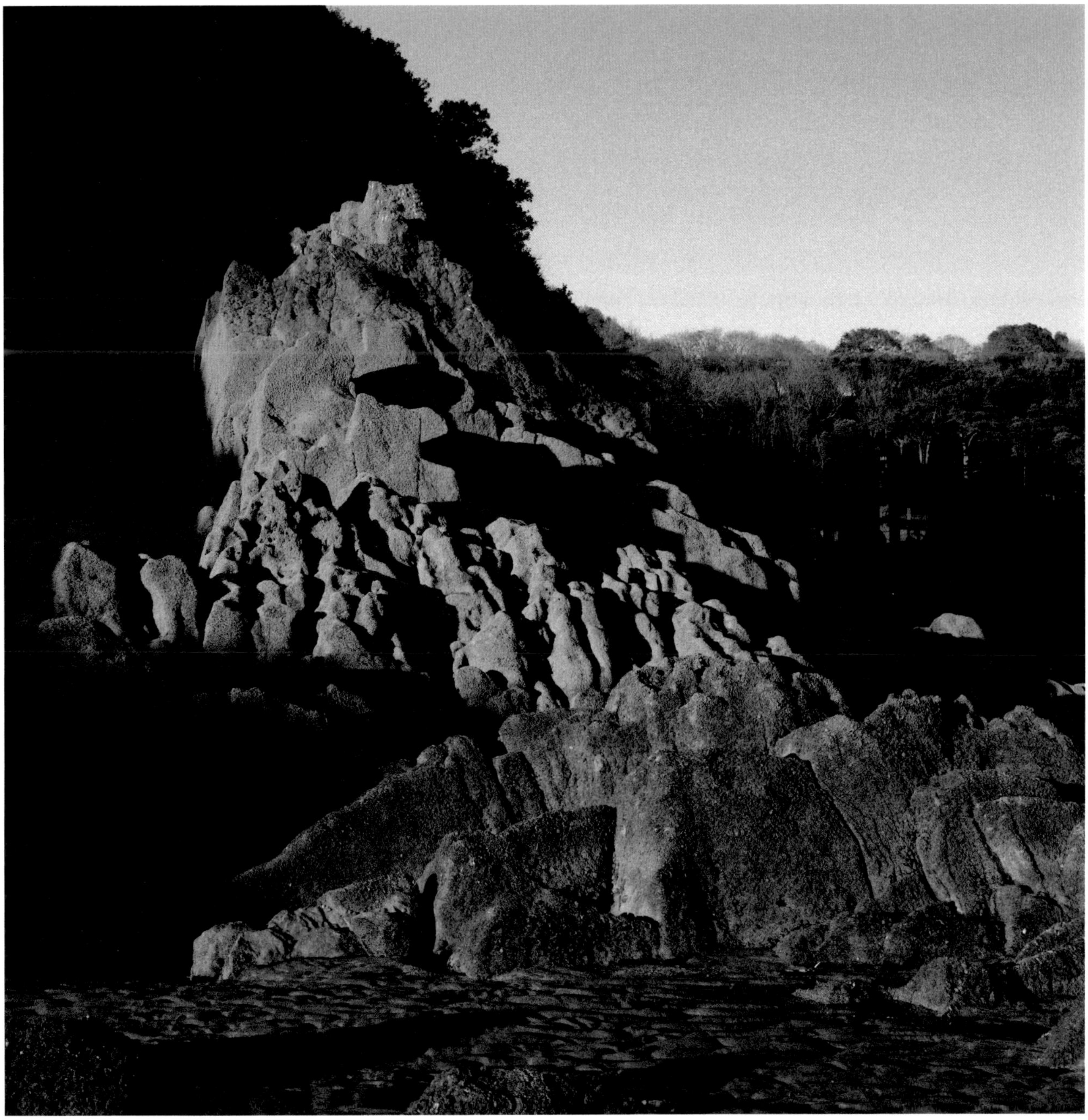

Caswell Bay (1), 2016

I'm in a car, a people carrier, and a giant bear
has its head pressed through the half open door.
It's inhaling deeply the air inside, and neither of us move.
I'm in danger, but it is so nice to be sniffed like that,
the dark unknown of his approach curtailed
by the mechanism of the sliding door
and the gentle force of my resistance against it.

THE CURIOUS MOANING OF KENFIG BURROWS

SOPHY RICKETT

GOST

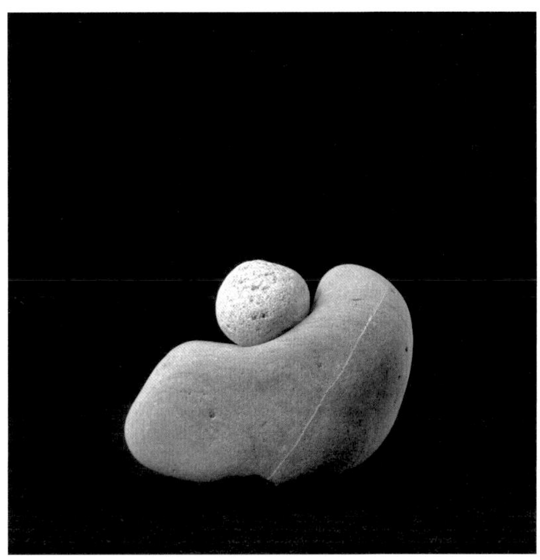

Stones, Kenfig Burrows, 2019

Fossilised Earbone of a Whale, 2018/2019

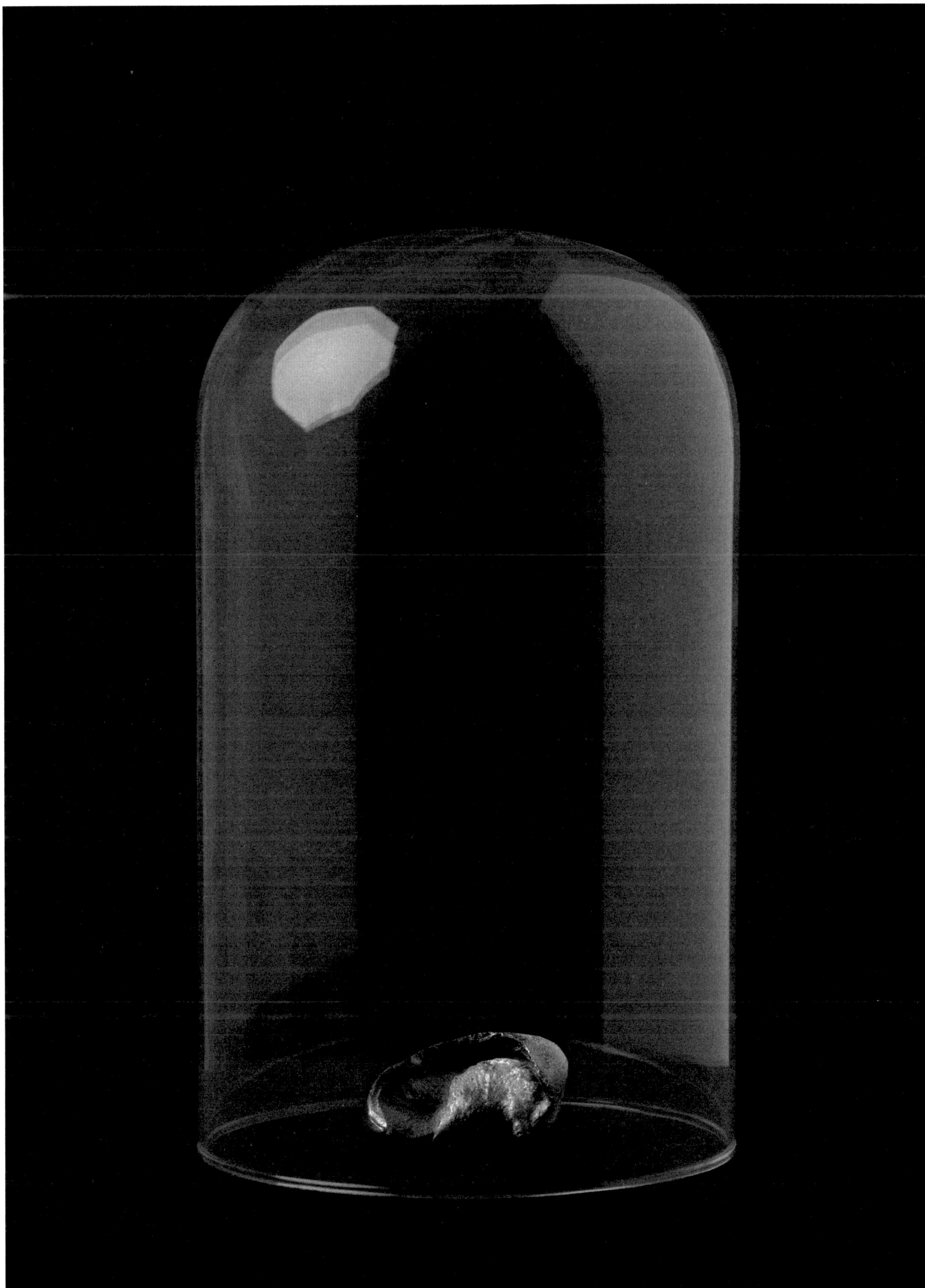

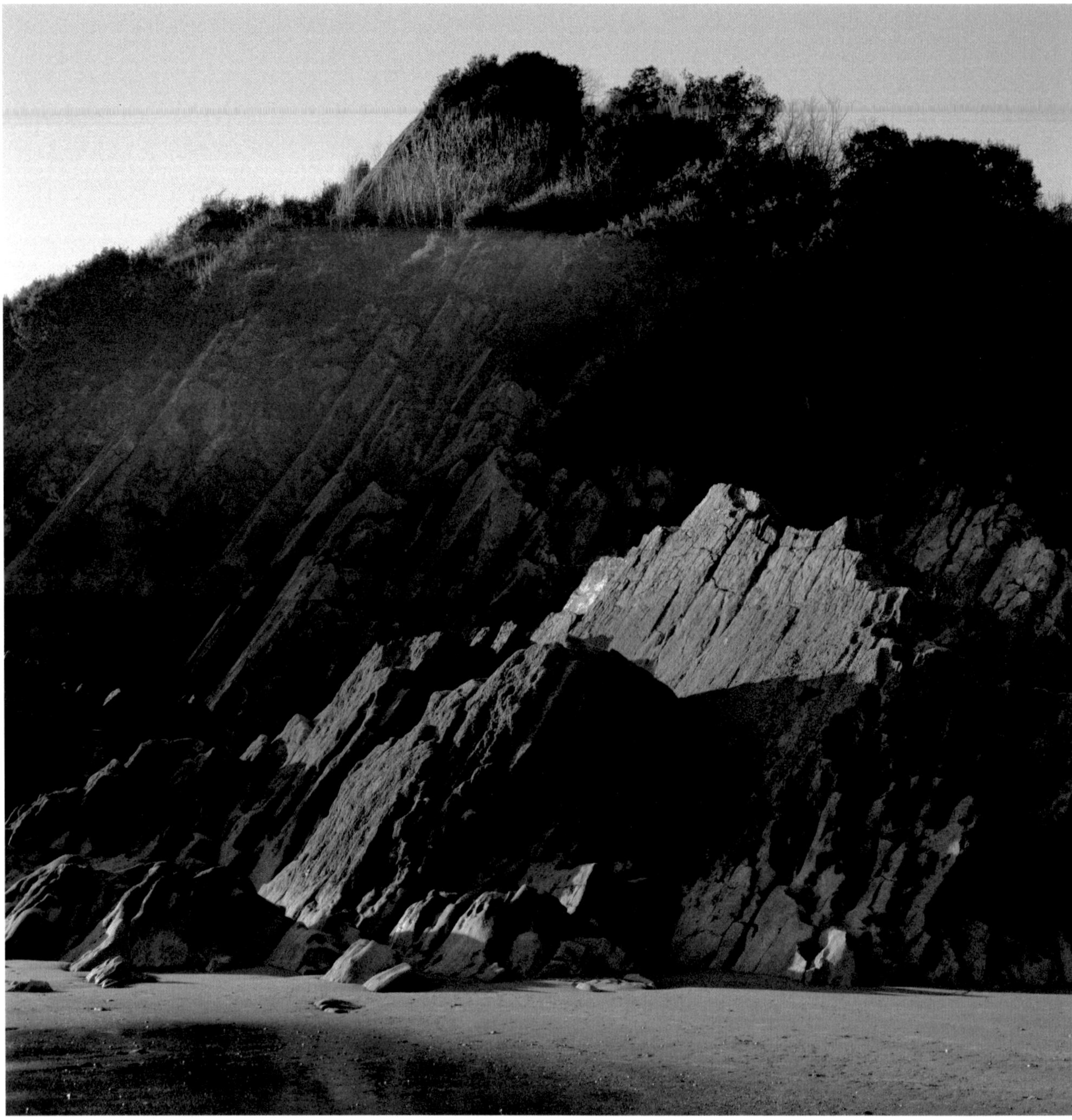

Caswell Bay (2), 2016

Where is it?

'Underneath the carpark at Caswell Bay,' comes the reply, and I think how I would like us to go there together, to discover it with her, be guided by her experience and understanding, her matter of factness, her warmth. I wait for her to continue but the subject tails off and I decide not to pursue it.

Later she mentions that she does not want to be featured in my project,
to appear in it in any way.

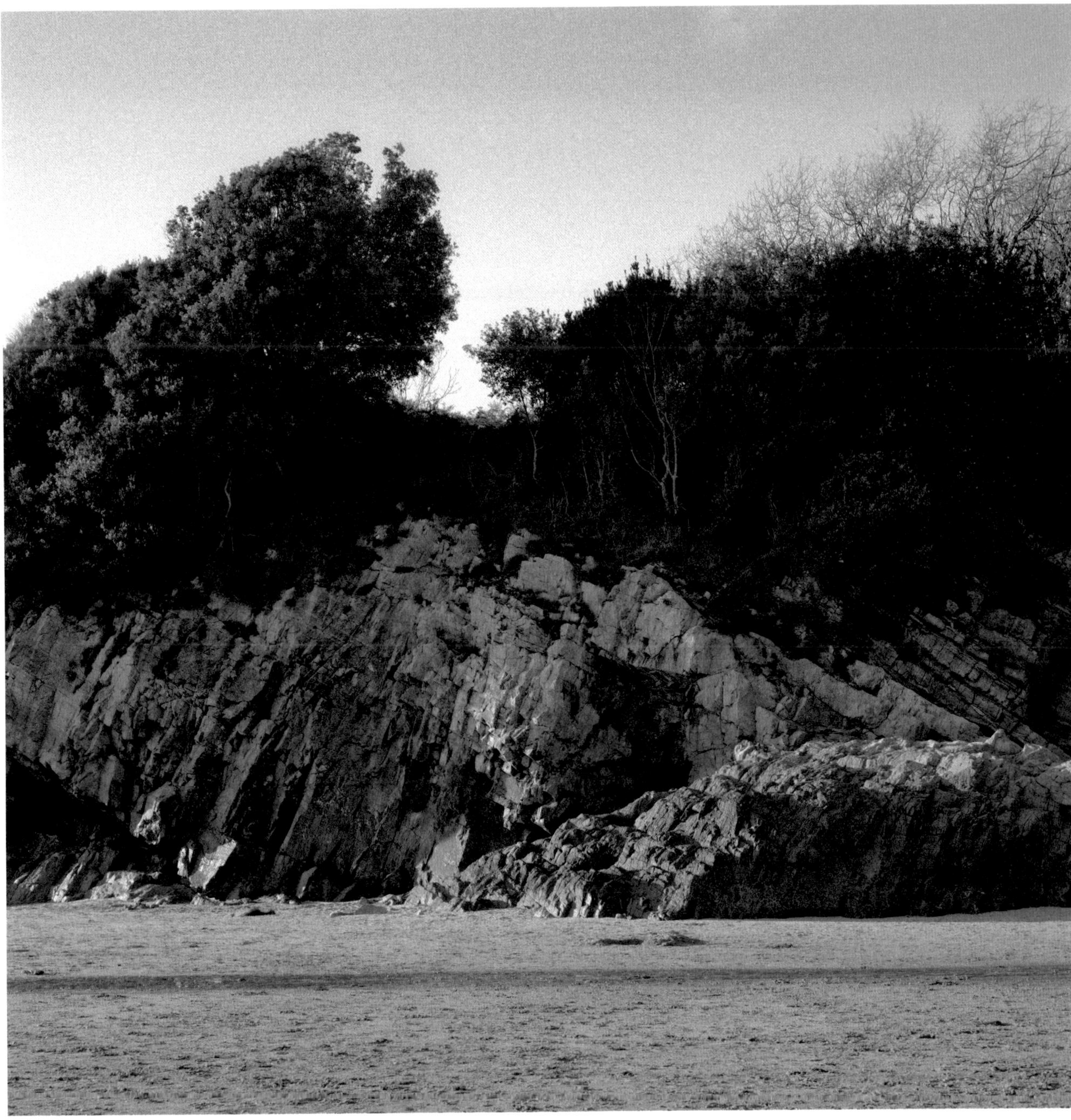

Caswell Bay (3), 2016

There are several photographs of the Caswell Bay house in the Dillwyn Llewelyn archive, part of which is held in a drably functional building on an industrial estate on the outskirts of Cardiff.

The house has been photographed looking inland from the beach; limestone marked moorland rising steeply up behind, black rectangles of the gabled roof windows suggestive of an empty interior. It's as if all the pictures have been taken on the same wintery day, variations on the same subject, a practice I recommend to my students.

'Take many exposures, keep moving around,' I might say towards the end of the day, as we sit at our patchwork of tables, tangles of plastic chairs lining the walls, black-out curtains hanging off their runners as they sway in the breeze.

Keep shifting your position in relation to your subject.

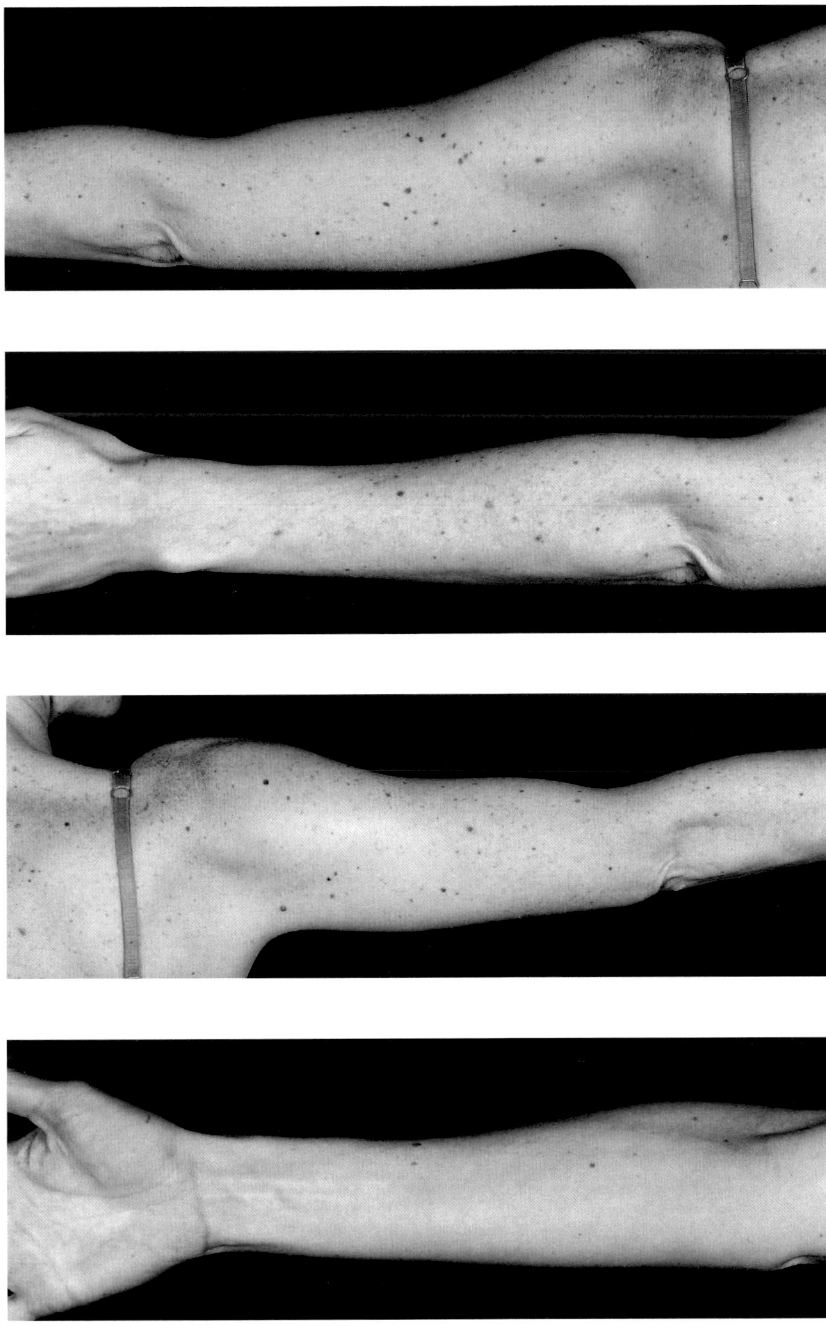

Young Woman/Observation (1), 1998/2019

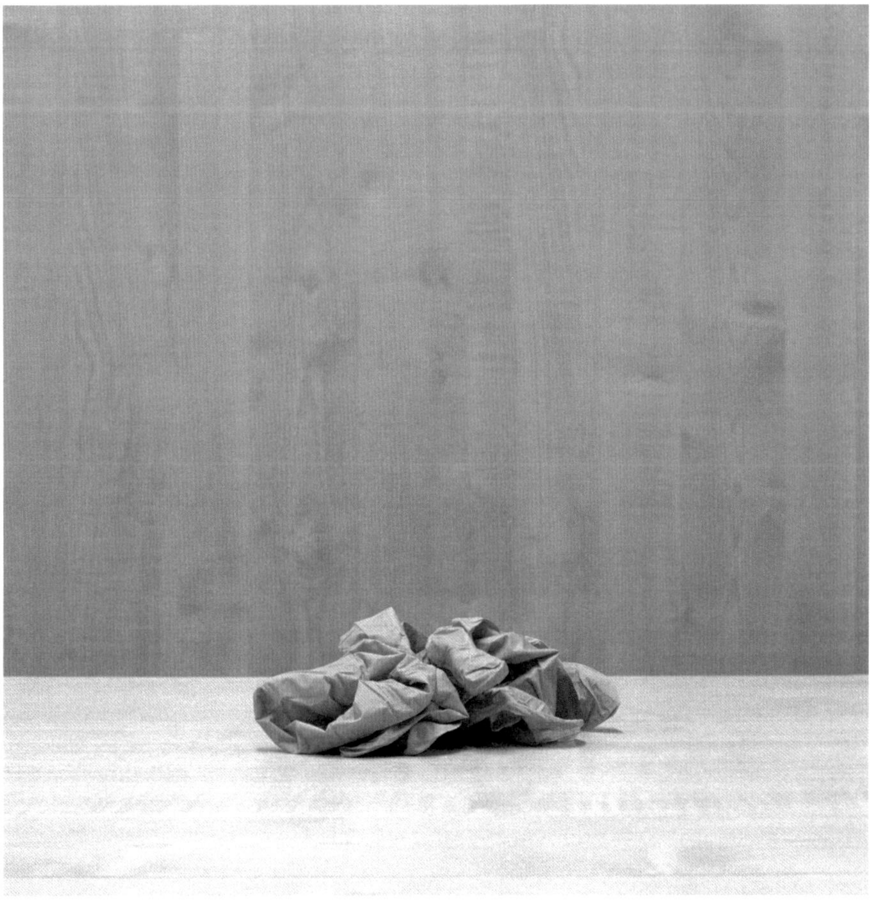

Gloves (archival handling), National Museum Wales, Cardiff, 2018

The house that's underneath the carpark is Caswell Cottage, and was built by John Dillwyn Llewelyn as a holiday home for his family. I look it up on Wikipedia, and read that Dillwyn Llewelyn's grandson, John Michael drowned there in 1878, aged twelve. Caswell Cottage was demolished in the 1960s, and the grounds concreted over to create the Caswell Bay carpark, a public facility managed by the City and County of Swansea.

I wonder how I can substantiate the details about Dillwyn Llewelyn's grandson, and feel weary at the prospect; the documents I will have to read, forms to fill in, appointments, acid free sleeves. Protective gloves.

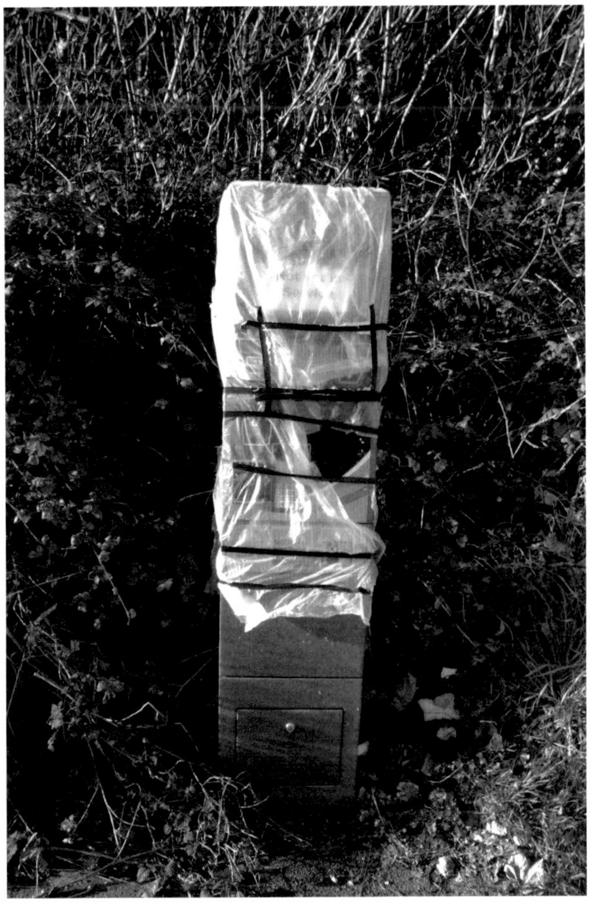

Carpark, Caswell Bay, 2018

Plastic Vase, Plastic Onions, National Museum Wales, Cardiff, 2018

Dillwyn Llewelyn took many photographs at Caswell Bay, some of which I encounter during my first time at the archive. The curator has anticipated my visit and on an oversized table in the viewing room, is a digitally reproduced version of every print in the collection, each mounted on a yellow index card.

Can we see the originals?

'Not today'

The cards are quietly passed around. I look, diligently, at each one, most of my objections internalised, but my attention is beginning to wander. I keep changing my mind about how I should be looking, what I should be looking for.

Should they stay in this order?

'Preferably. But don't worry if they get a little bit muddled up.'

The images are already in a muddle; I can't find the continuity, the chronology, and they are sequenced in an order that only seems to make sense numerically. Information comes anecdotally, many of our questions have answers unknown.

The family pursued their interest in photography collectively; some of the images, we are told, might have been incorrectly attributed to John, rather than his wife Emma, sister Mary, or daughter Thereza. They were as experimental with subject matter as they were with process; family portraits, some formal, some more relaxed are combined with topographical studies of rock formations, historical buildings and scenes in and around Penllergare and Caswell Bay. They staged elaborate pictorial tableaux, using props, costumes and pet dogs to reconstruct scenes from books and legend. They experimented with scale, photographing snowflakes, and then the moon. They made prints from each other's negatives, developed darkroom techniques; dodging out and burning in areas of the image to produce a greater tonal range.

But I'm finding it all quite difficult to process and perhaps by way of compensation, from time to time, I take my camera and make a picture of one of the reproductions, stimulated more by what I know than by what is new.

A capture, but also, a refusal.

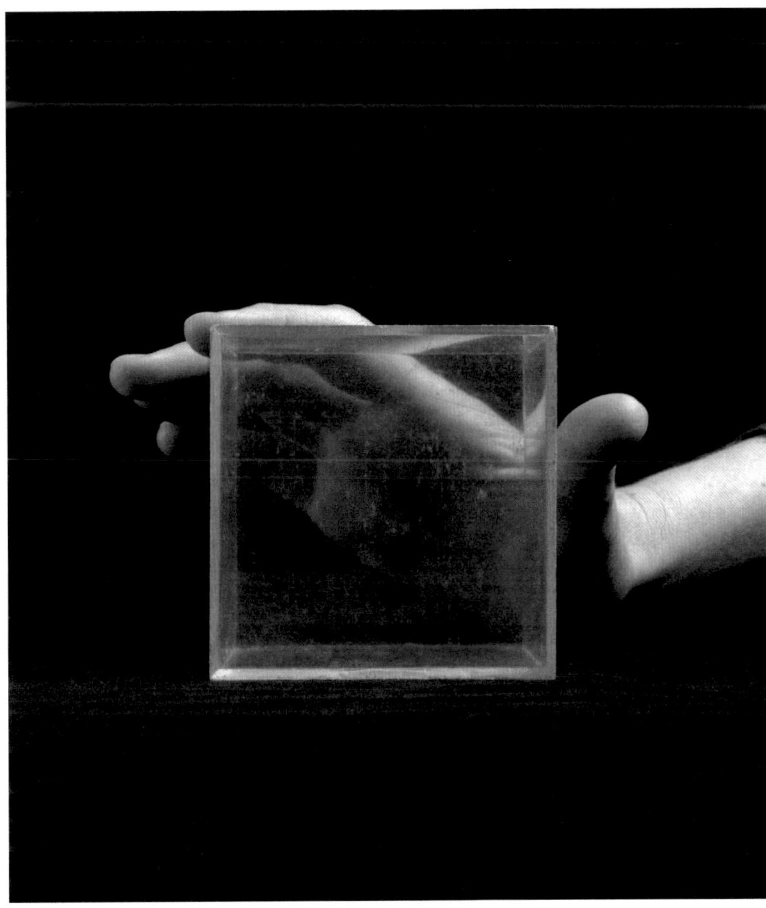

Photocube, 2018

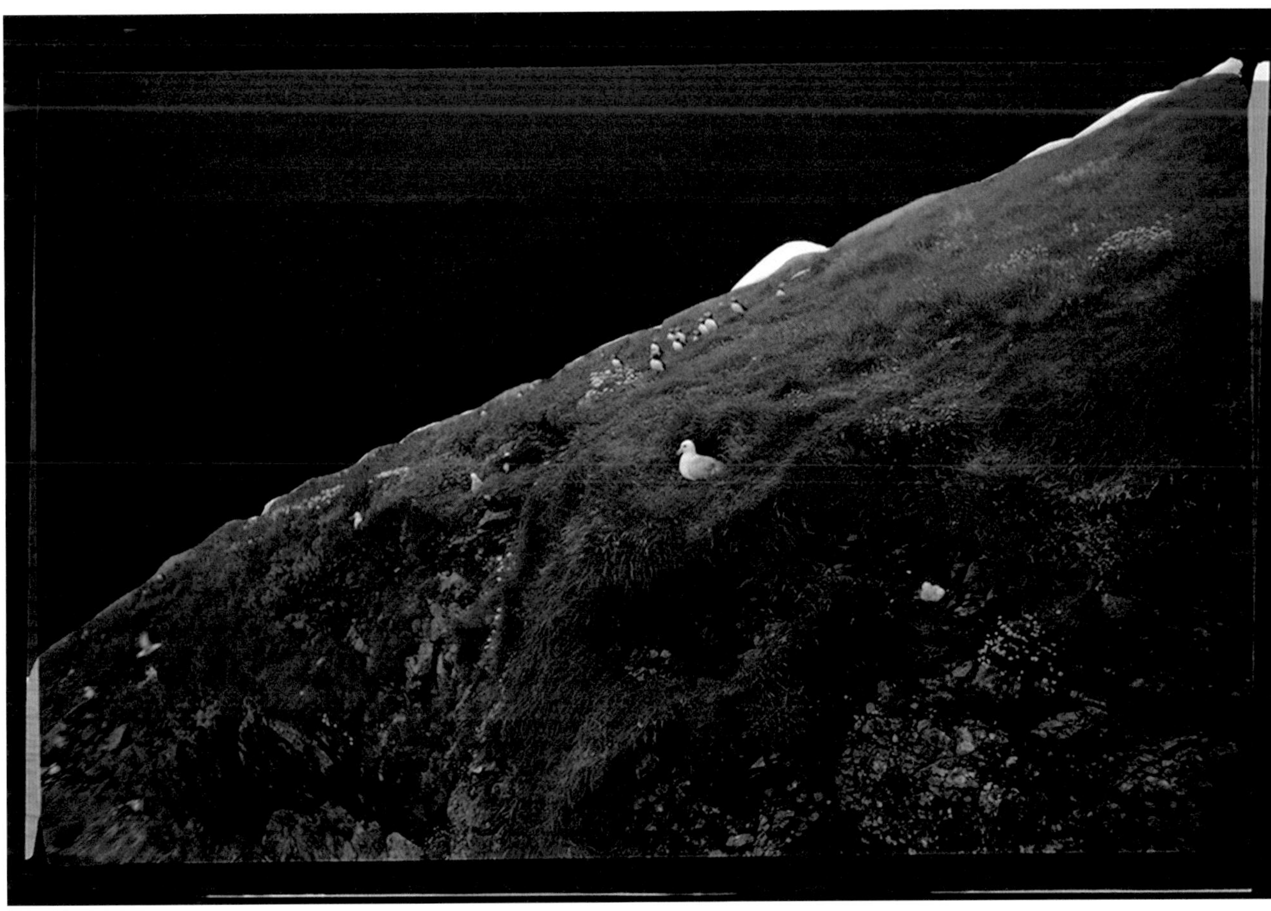

St Kilda, 1964/2017

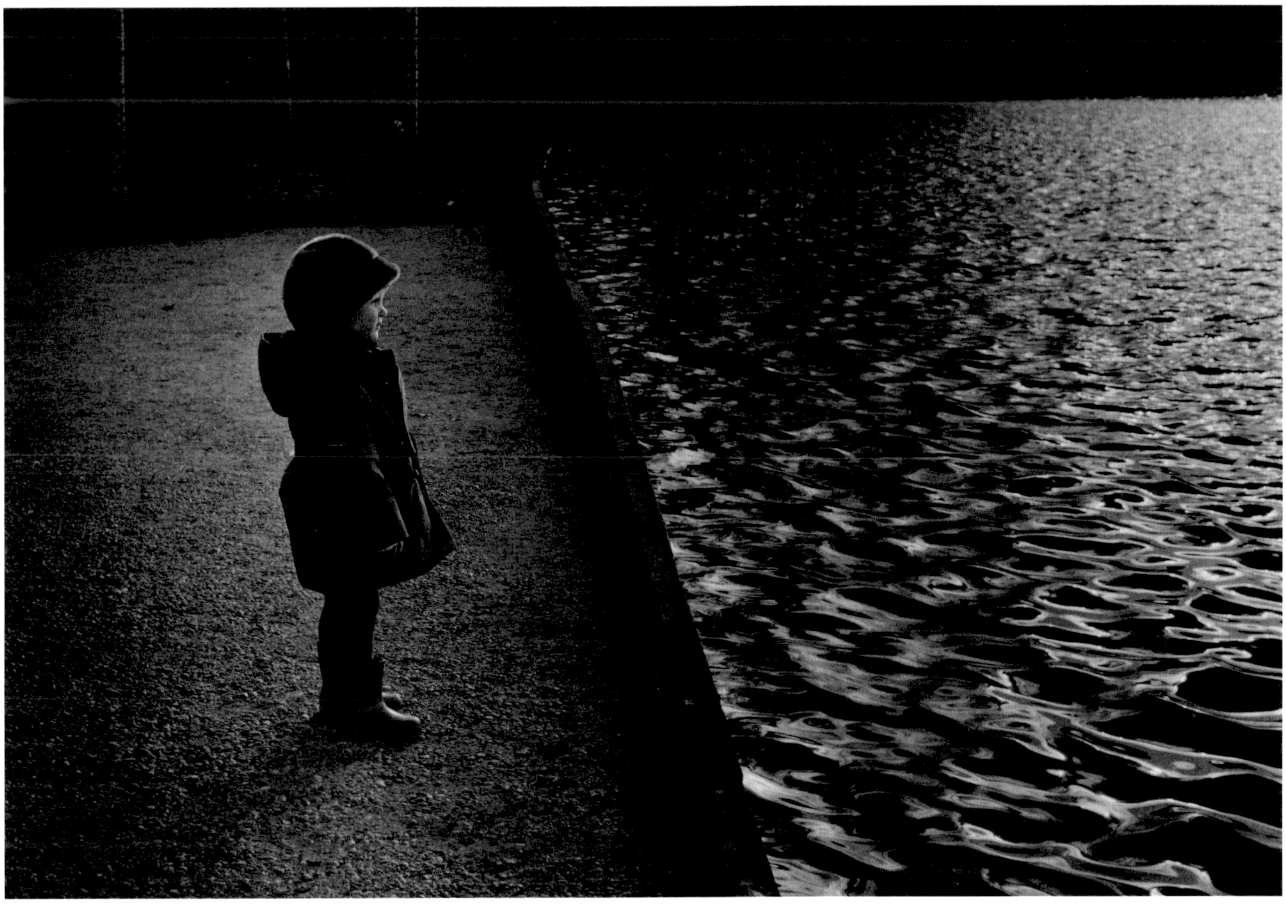

Young Girl, 1973/2019

Here is a picture of a woman on a beach.

It's Thereza and she is standing with a telescope, looking out to sea. She holds the device delicately, the eyepiece held in place with her right hand, her left hand gently supporting the extended weight of the optical tube.

There is something incongruous about her Victorian dress, but of course it makes sense and there are other details I find even more intriguing; that this young woman, a photographer, a scientist, with her aptitude, her talent, her opportunity and her inquisitiveness, is also a beloved daughter, subject of, and also subject to her father's scrutinizing gaze.

There are two versions of the same scene, one showing the cliffs in the background, the other more tightly cropped, the tide a bit further out. I think about the time between the exposures, the technical adjustments, the dialogue between them. The pictures were made at Caswell Bay in 1853 when Thereza was 19; three years before she started writing the diary that, 160 years later, I would discover, packed away, in an acid free box in the climate controlled environment of the British Library's Manuscripts and Archives Reading Room.

Thereza was John and Emma's eldest child, and many of the anecdotes about the family refer to the closeness of the relationship between father and daughter; their shared interest in science and photography, that the observatory at Penllergare was built to encourage her passion for astronomy and how she helped him with his photographic experiments. The collection is also known for the quality of its family portraits; Mary's photograph of Thereza's brother Willy is thought to be the first time a smile was captured on film. Many of the portraits have a spontaneity and warmth unusual for their era and Penllergare is portrayed as a productive, lively and happy family home.

But something else sticks with me more. Something about Thereza's presence in the stories that have built up around the collection, something about her role as an assistant, facilitator, mentor, muse.

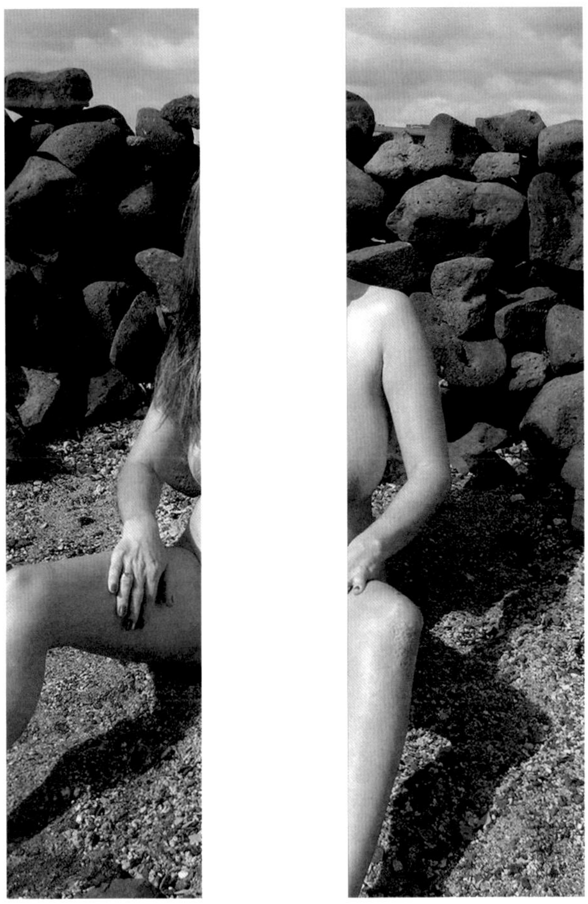

Woman on a Beach, 2017/2018

A story starts to come to life, but is obfuscated by anecdote, by the way certain narratives dominate, determined by the arbitrariness of who, or what survived.

The house at Penllergare was demolished in the 60s, and council offices built on the site. While the observatory survived, the gardens fell into disrepair. The irrigation system failed, the roof of the orchid house fell in, the lake stagnated, the boathouse collapsed. People broke in, rode their bikes, lit fires, took drugs. The plans of the house and gardens were destroyed in a fire, bundles of lantern slides abandoned in a ditch.

And slowly the connection between subject, photograph, photographer begins to fall away; so much destruction, some casual, some by accident, just as it is about to become interesting, just as it is about to be missed.

Some of Thereza's diaries and papers are held in the British Library and I go there to read them. I switch between her diaries and memoirs, drawn into the separation between the two testimonies, written by the same hand, sixty-seven years apart. The diaries detail her day-to- day life; walks, marine curiosities found on the beach, the comings and goings of family, her developing interest in photography.

She writes about a drop of milk, seen under a microscope, describing it as 'a thin fluid, thickly filled with opaque white globules'; a distinction drawn between the appearance of a substance to the naked eye and something more essential that can only be inferred through the lens of a microscope.

The memoir is more reflective, evoking a different sense of time, an awareness of her family's place in the history of photography, the burden of significance, the struggle to recall: 'It must have been my mother, who taught me to read.'

The diary starts on May 3rd, Thereza's twenty-second birthday. She was given a camera by her father, although doesn't write about using it until the autumn of that year, around the time of her engagement, when for several weeks, he suffered with a series of violent headaches that left him unable to leave the house.

My father, a doctor, gave me my first camera when I was fifteen. The first photographs I took before then were with a camera belonging to him; a bulky tool with an oversized popper on its brown leather case. He kept it in his study, in a cupboard that held other types of instruments, some dusty, some new, but apart from a stethoscope they were things without names, purposeful things, to do with his work, to do with looking inside.

Wikipedia again:
'An otoscope is a medical device, which is used to look into the ear.'

I can still feel my family doctor describing the appearance of my eardrum, the source of all that pain, and the seepage of watery fluid that would stain the faded blue velvet cushion to which I pressed my poorly ear. My mum was worried I would go deaf with so many infections:

'My mother went deaf with her mastoids...'

I have never seen inside an ear, I can only imagine it, through his description, breathed into the side of my face as he gently pulls at the lobe of my ear. 'Oh yes, very sore... red... flaky.... lacerated drum... pus.... Is that very tender?'... as the cold metal device was pressed deep into the hot canal.

And I would have nodded shyly that yes it was. 'Tender' is quite right; a word that can describe such differences in sensation, both given and received.

Years later my dad will go deaf and, for a while, the communication between us will completely break down.

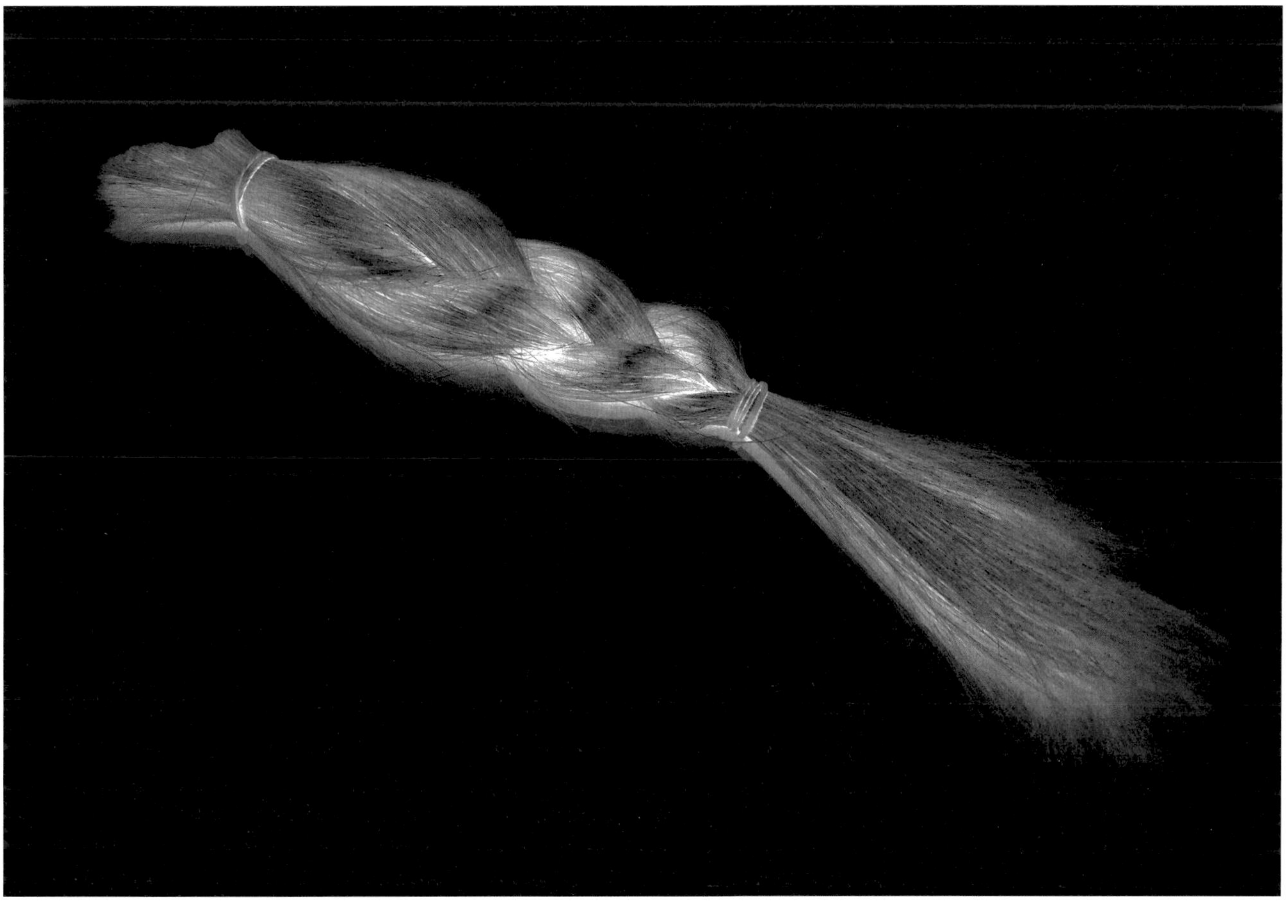

Plait, 2015/2019

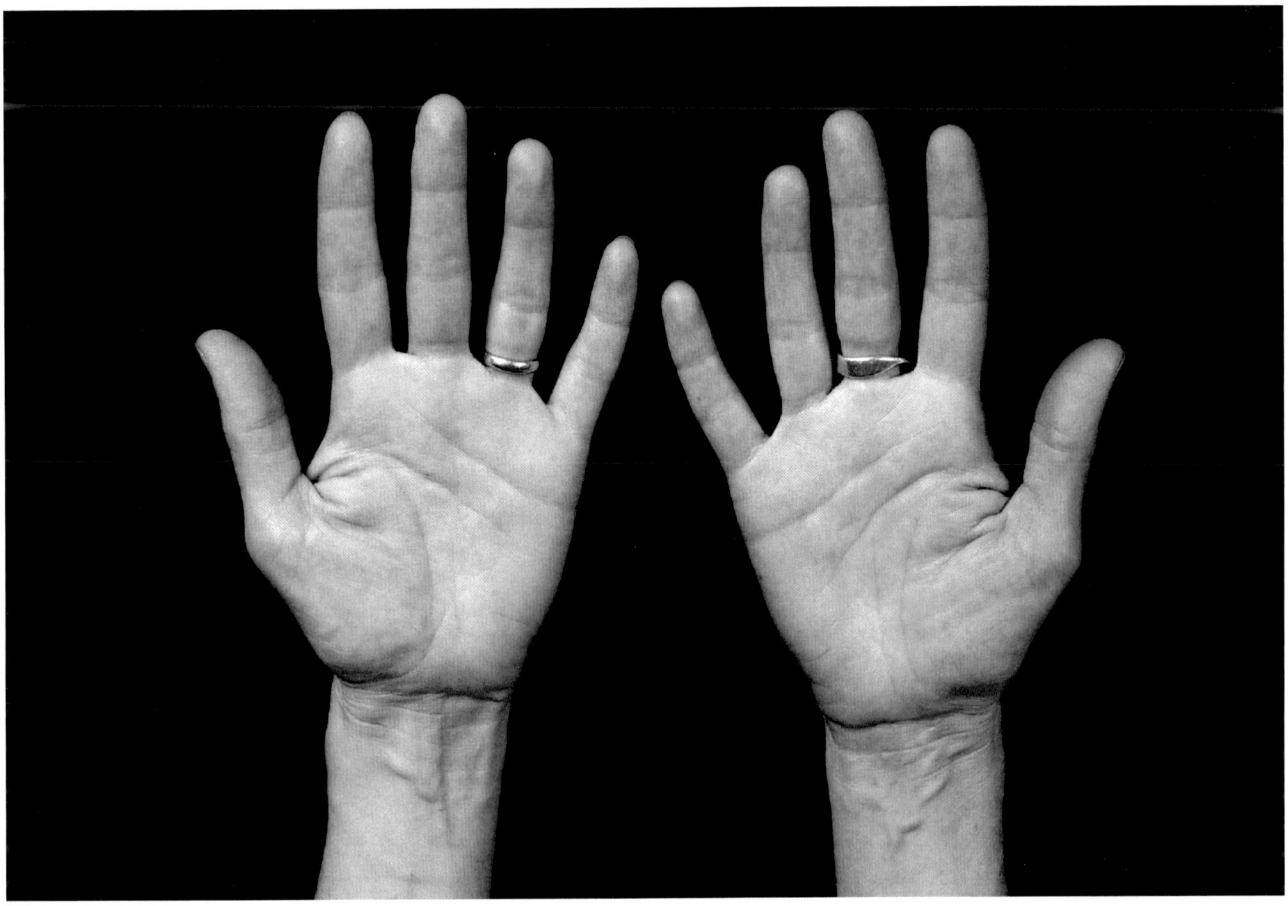

Young Woman/Observation (2), 1998/2019

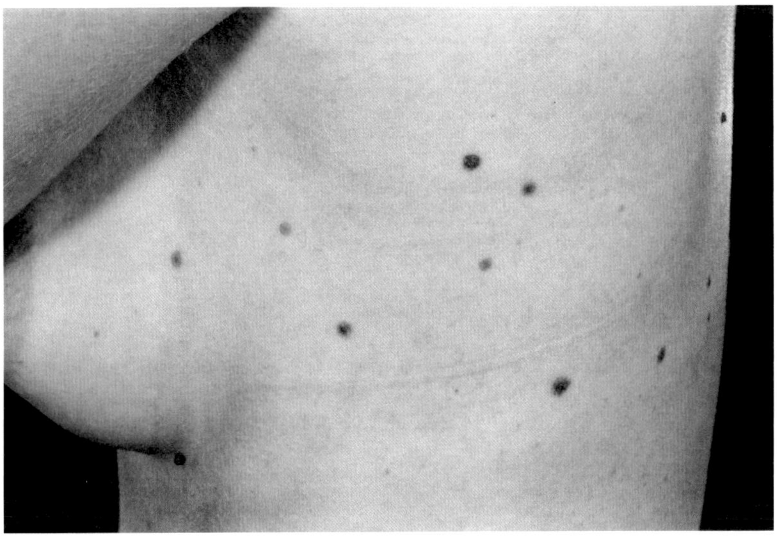

Young Woman/Observation (3), 1998/2019

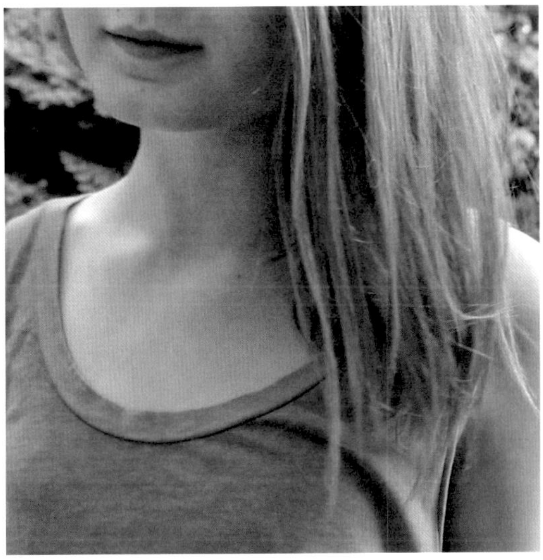

Girl, 2015/2019

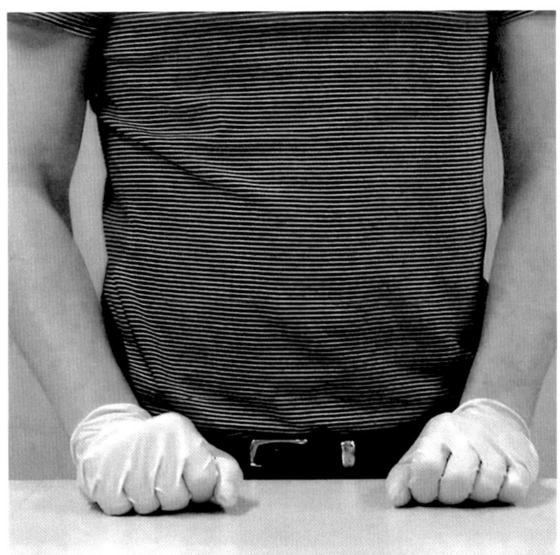

Archivist (2), Photographic Collections, National Museum Wales, Cardiff, 2016

The carpark at Caswell Bay is long and thin, fitting Thereza's description of it as a 'strip of land with a good garden, already there.' The plot runs perpendicular to the beach, the white painted parking bays all facing forwards, towards the sea. In a shady corner is a visitor's information panel, with its own little damp roof, spongy green swards of moss.

The faded text has a helpful, hopeful tone, multiple imperatives driving it forward, familiar in both senses of the word; climb the cliffs, enjoy the view, spot the lizards, take some time, notice the ancient oak. And then, a change of register, 'The only evidence of the estate today are a few garden plant escapees in the woodland and the coach house, which is now the Countryside Centre.'

In the library, weeks later, I find a list made by Thereza, of trees planted after the cottage was built. The Nothofagus betuloides (an evergreen beech) had thrived in the warm microclimate of the bay, and by 1878 was seventeen feet high and attracted 'great attention from botanists.'

But as I stand there looking up into the thick canopy of evergreens and conifers, seeking material echoes of that past; nothing.

The tide that afternoon is at its lowest, flat sands stretching to the west, shimmering pools of shallow water, the bright glare of the Bristol Channel in the distance. I recognize the rocks from the pictures of Thereza with her telescope. The concrete of the sea defence is a gentle slope etched with deep vertical ridges. The river emerges from a drainage outlet that runs under the road, similar—in engineering terms at least—to the outlet of the River Llan as it enters the 'picturesque landscape of Penllergare'; a landscape which, according to one of the anecdotes I will hear many times, is 'topsliced' by the M4 motorway.

Further east along the M4, is Margam Castle, home of Thereza's uncle. The house was built on the side of Margam Mountain, a bleak landscape dissected and indented by ravines and rivers, small wooded valleys and black peat bogs.

From that high up position overlooking the bay, they would know when a storm was approaching from the sound of the wind whistling up from Kenfig Burrows, a 'curious moaning' that was, according to her uncle, Kenfig Burrows 'talking' to Margam Mountain. It's a striking image; a landscape in dialogue with itself, the way it evokes the physical contours of the valley, the geological terrain, the 'Legend of Margam.'

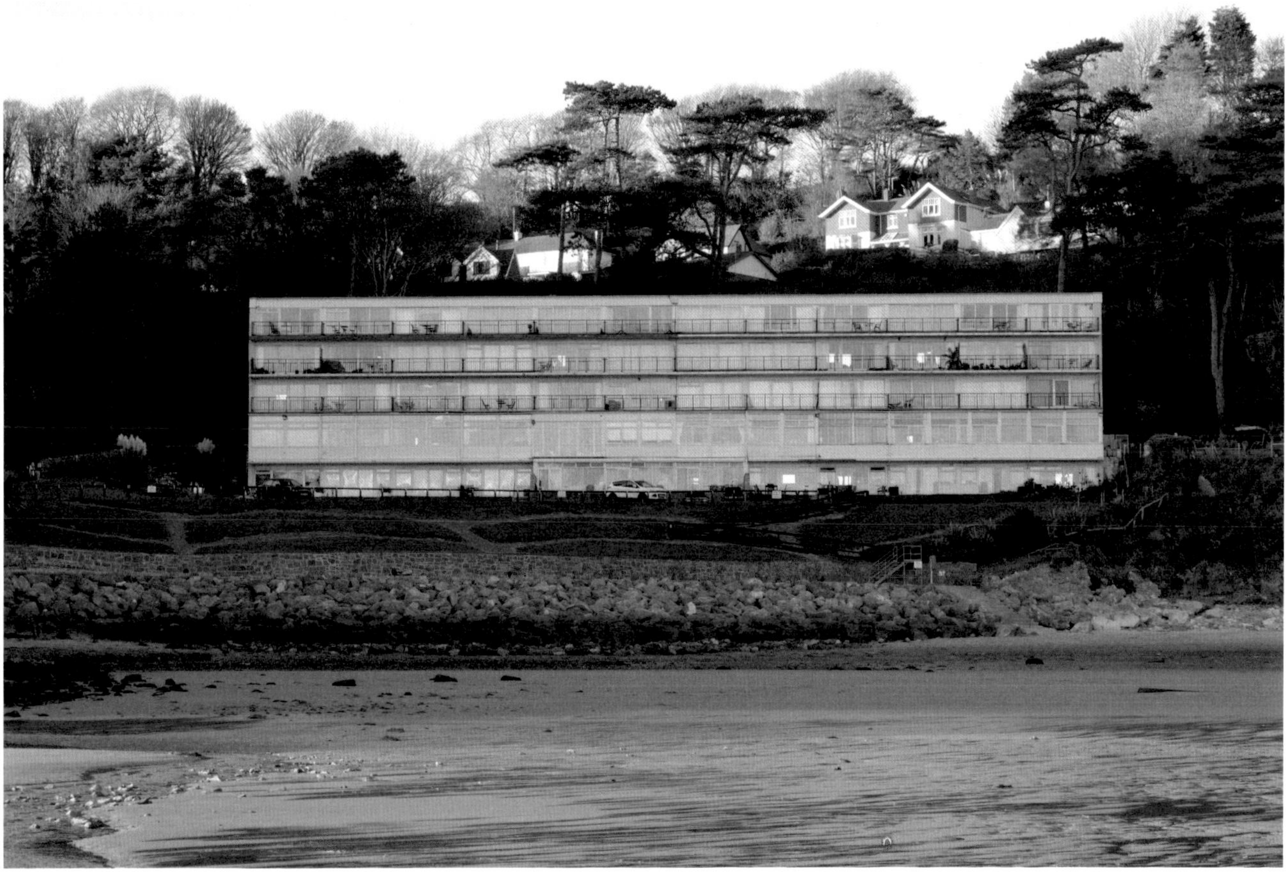

Apartments, Caswell Bay, 2016

Following spread
Tree (divided), Margam Mountain, 2019

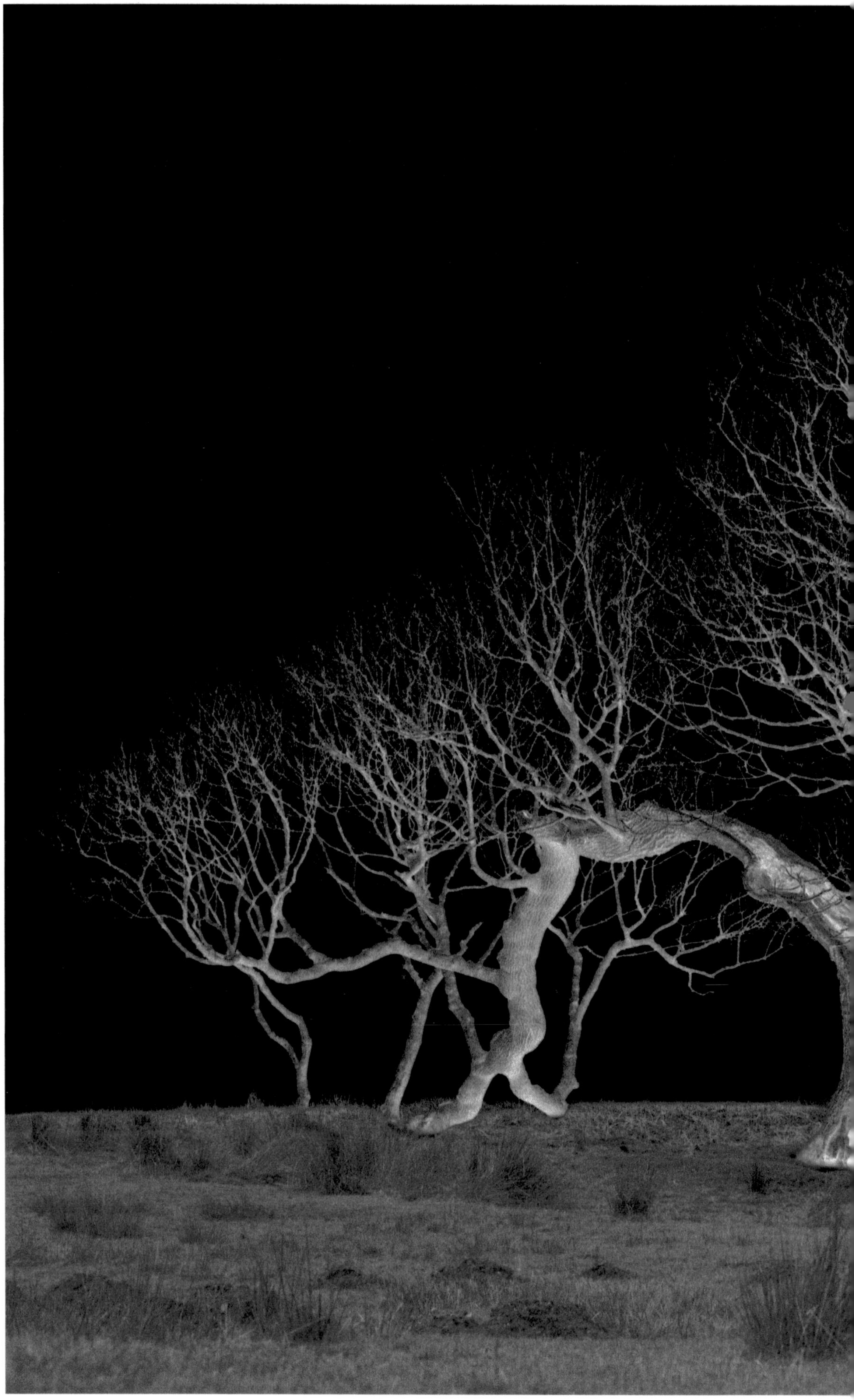

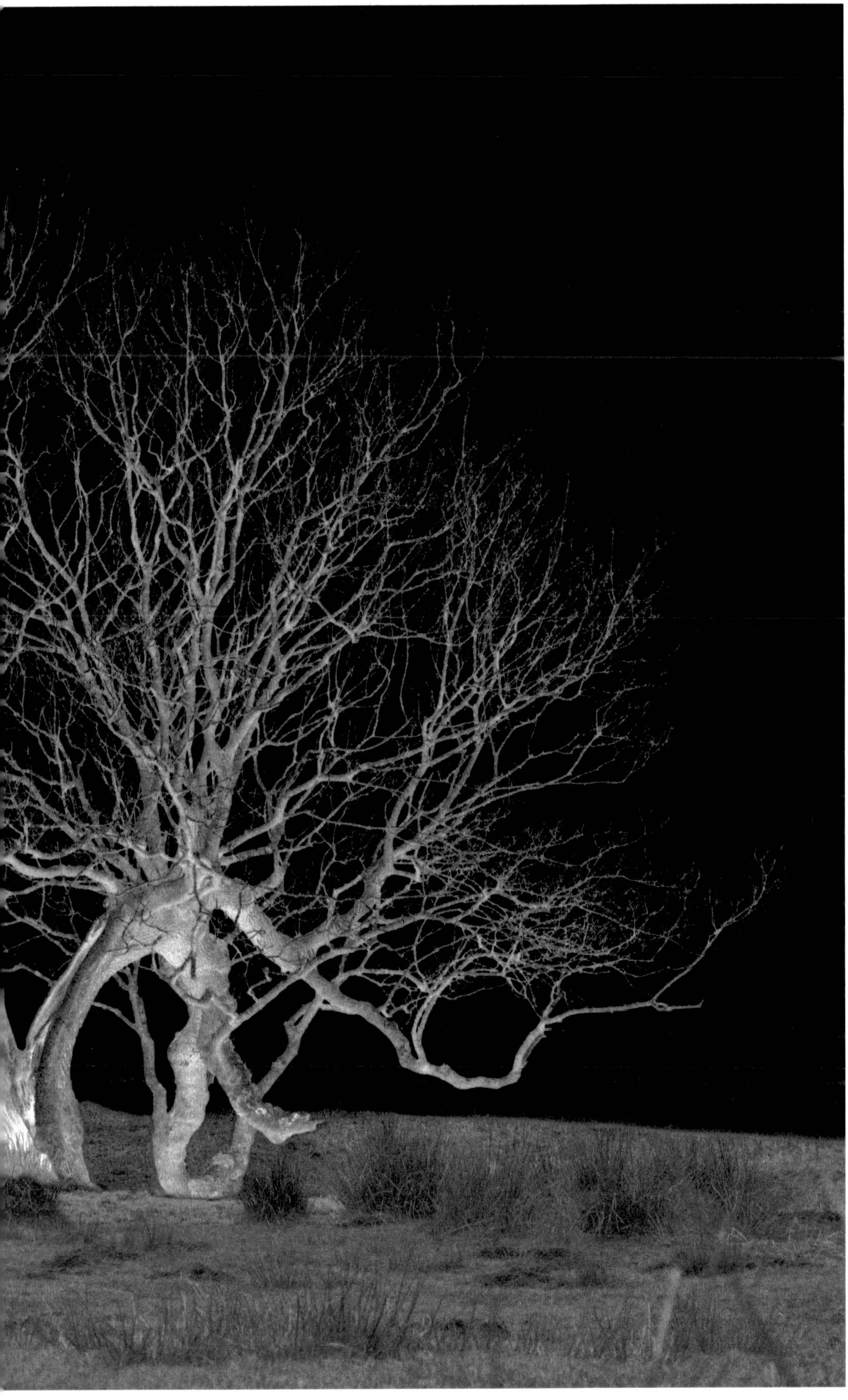

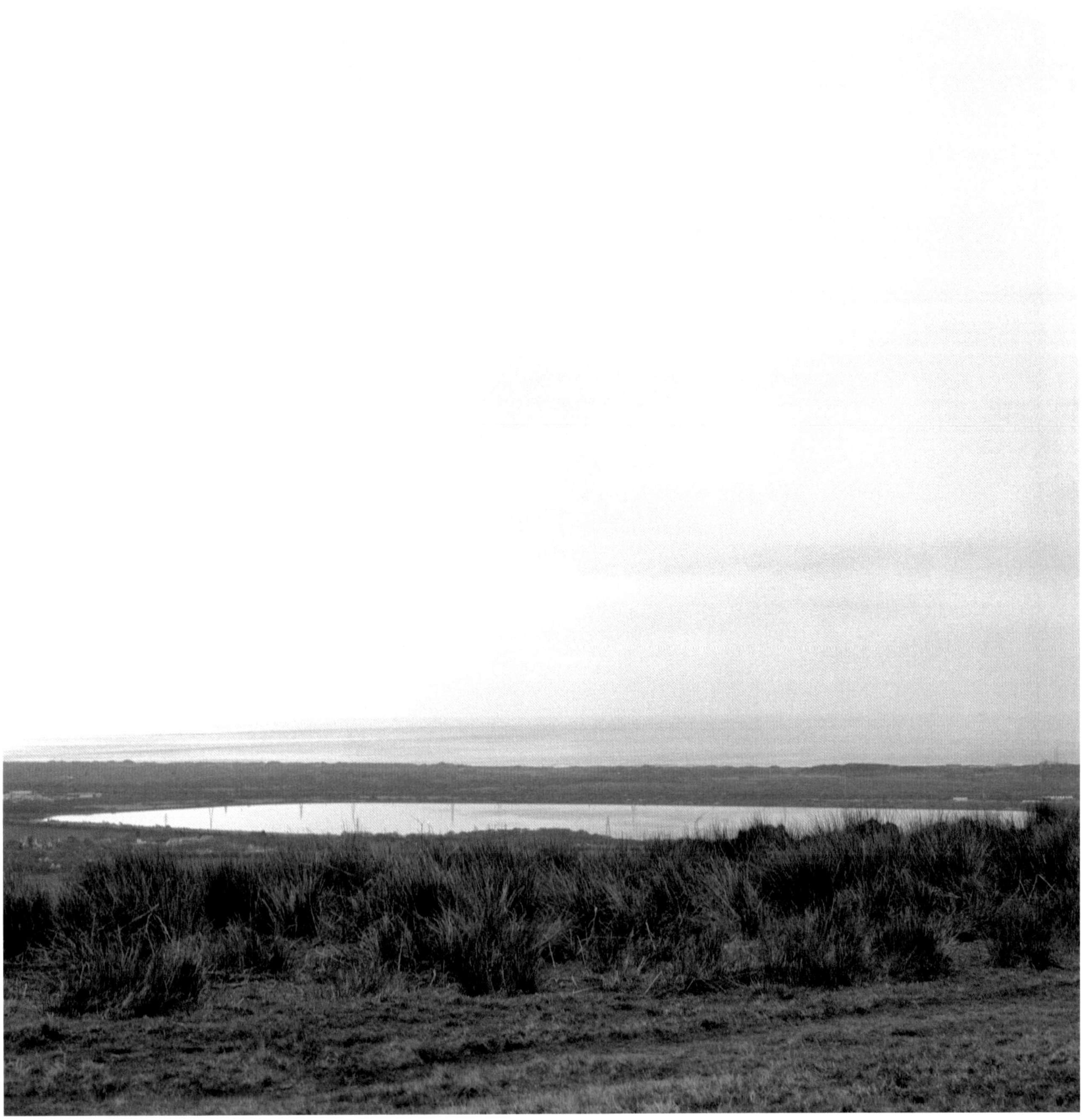

Kenfig Pool from Margam Mountain, 2019

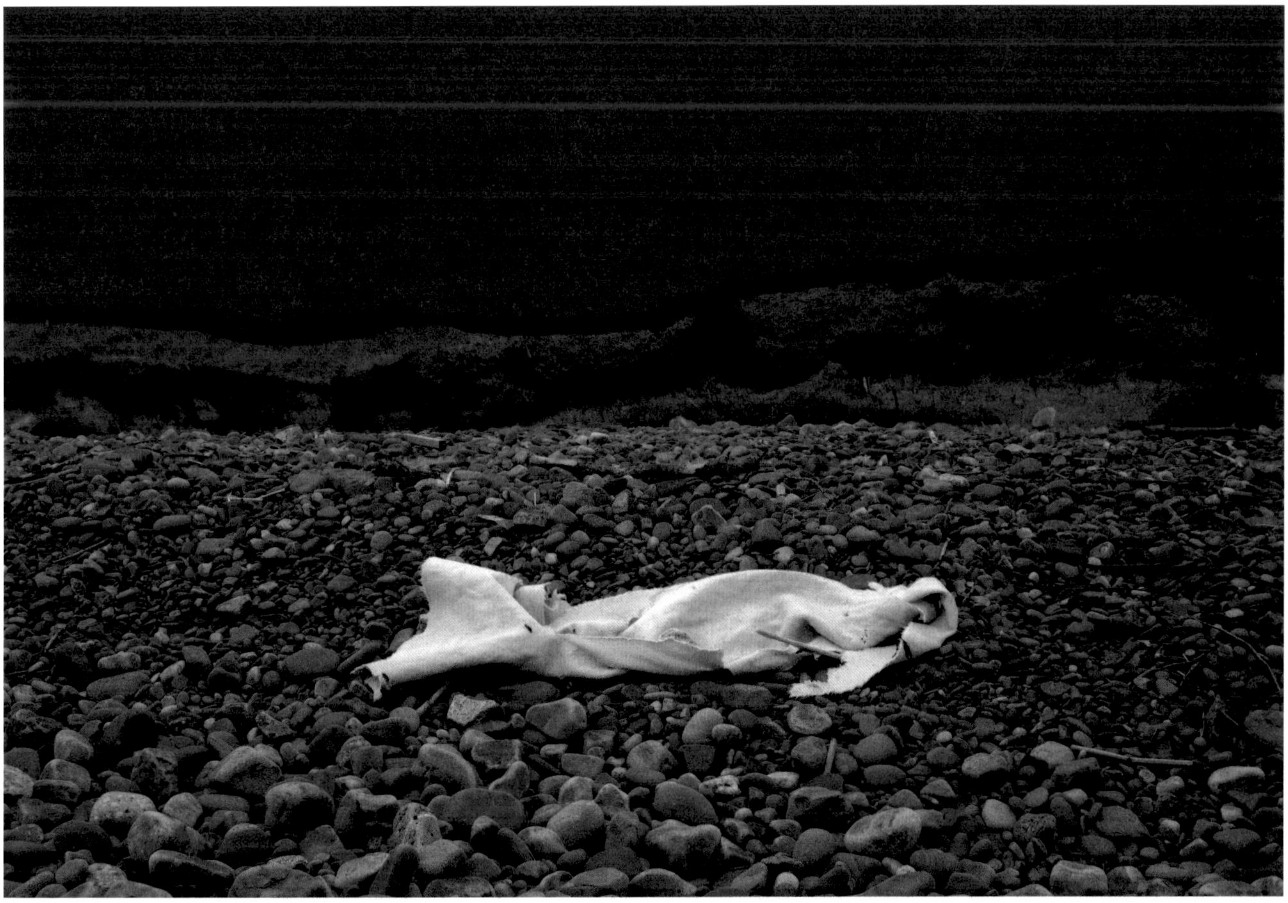

Cream Felt (marine curiosity), Kenfig Burrows, 2018

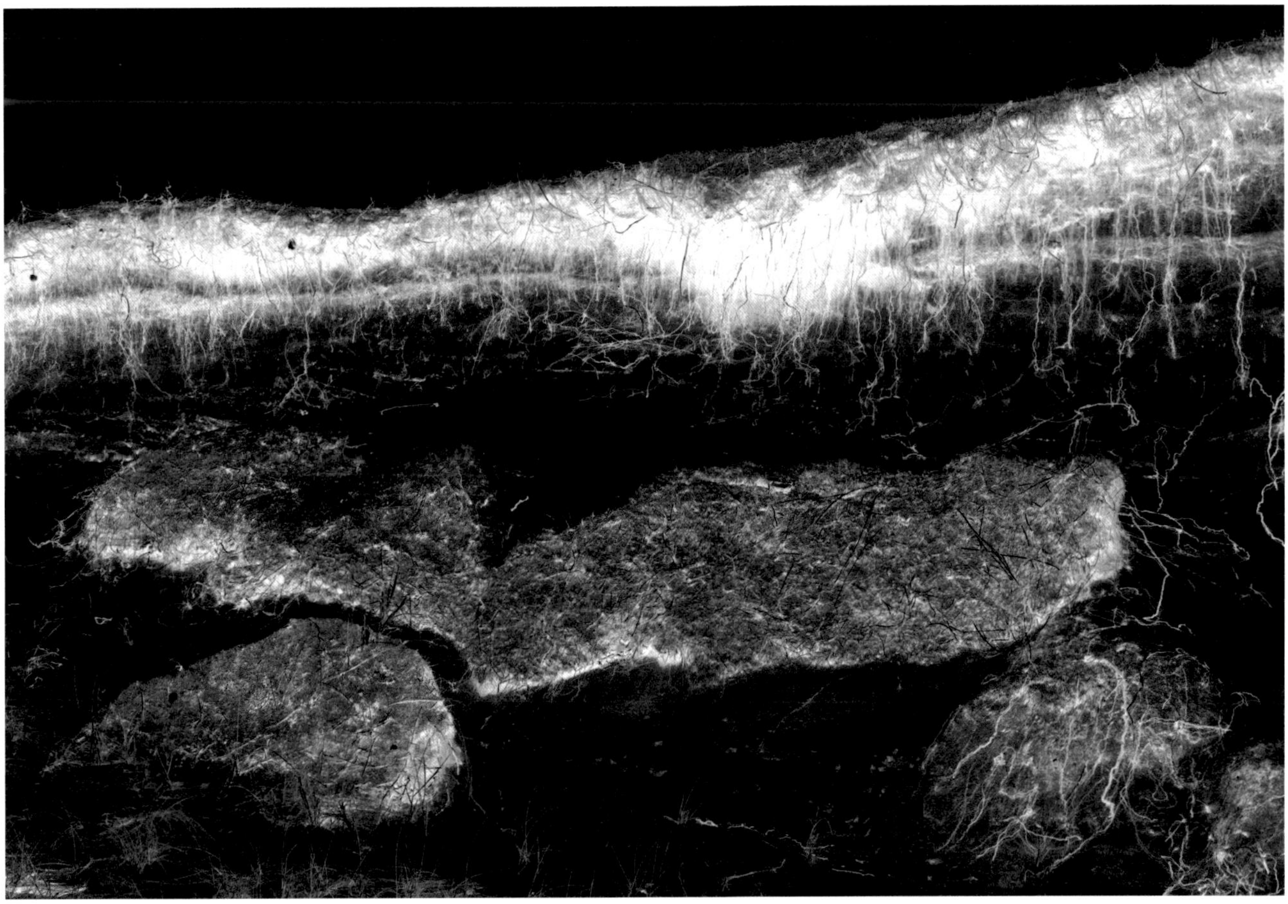

Coastal Edge (cross section), Kenfig Burrows, 2019

I find out that Kenfig Burrows is now a nature reserve, managed by Bridgend County Council. There used to be a website, but its funding was cut. I find reviews of the beach in an online walker's guide:

> 'I found both water and beach to be of a reasonable standard ideal for sunbathing and a swim when the tide is in. The fact that it is isolated makes it the perfect place for both male and females.'
>
> 'The wife and I spent a very pleasant couple of hours here Sunday afternoon. It's quite a trek through the nature reserve to get to the beach, but once there it's very quiet and peaceful. There were a couple of other unclothed men on the beach and one guy seemed to take a particular interest in my wife. I don't know if it's normal for men to stare at women but it seemed a bit rude. It didn't worry us and we enjoyed ourselves anyway... '
>
> 'GREAT BEACH! Came here midweek the beach was lovely. Walked naked along the designated beach. Had no problems with the usual ogling... Probably about ten other nudes on the beach—didn't see any textiles.'

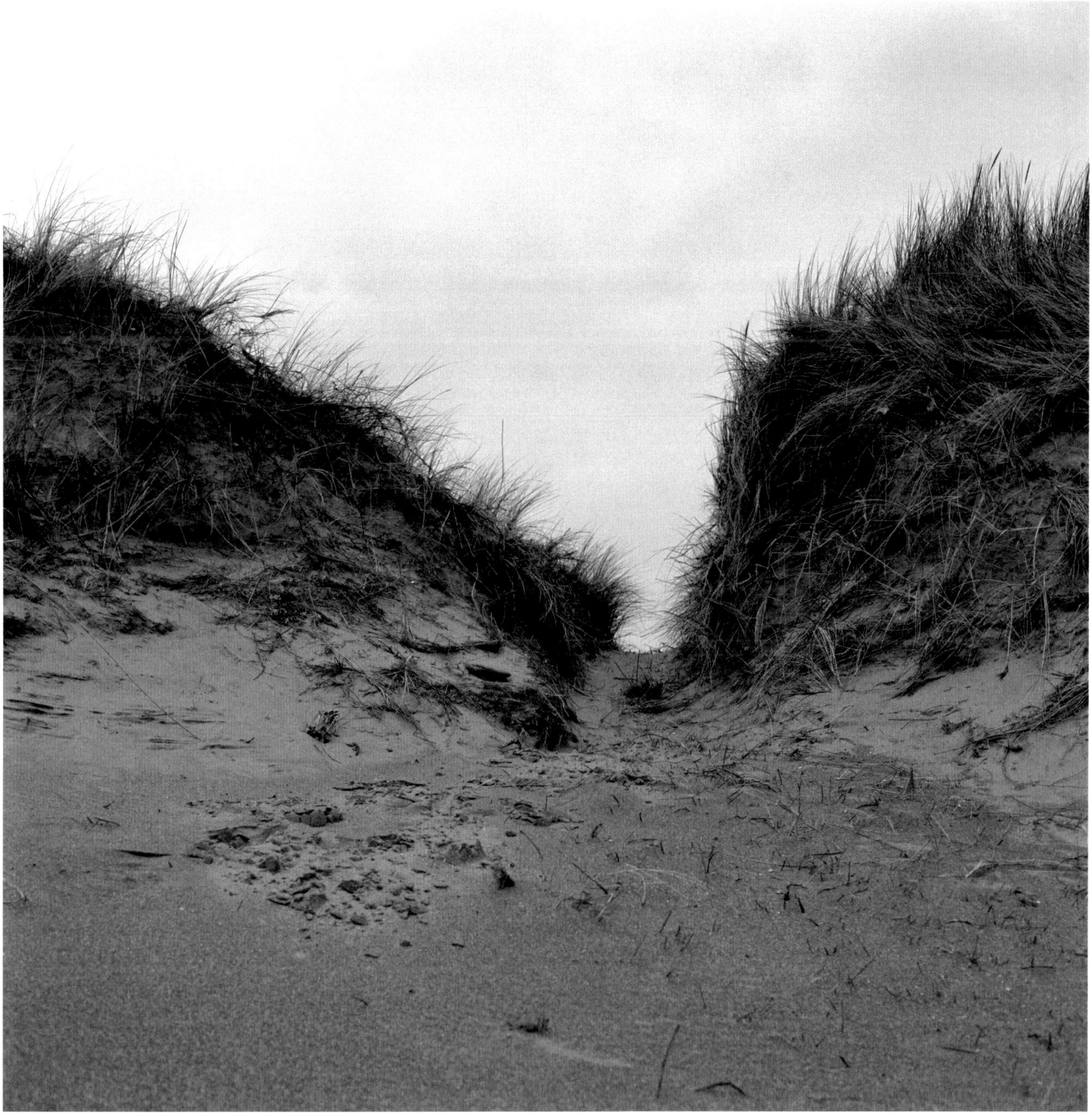

Dunes, Kenfig Burrows, 2019

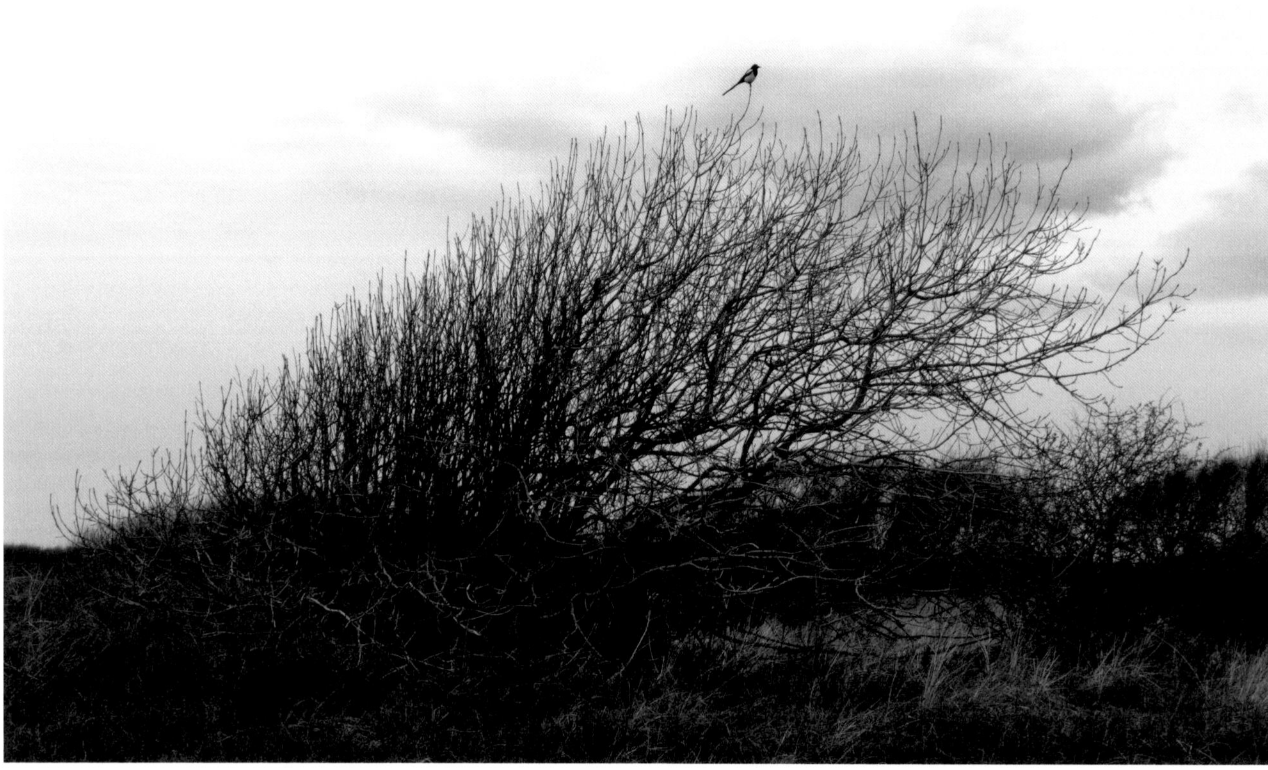

Tree, Kenfig Burrows, 2019

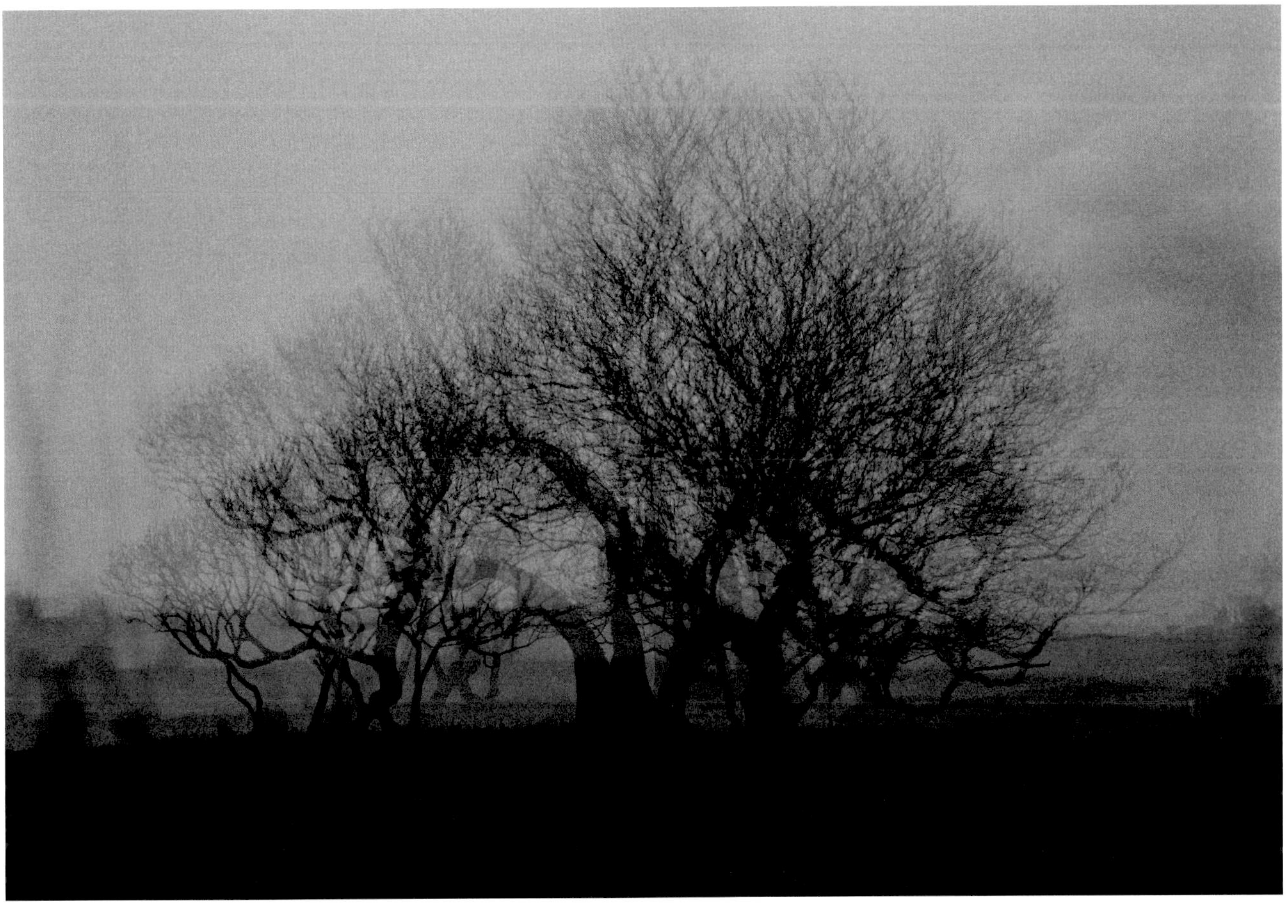

Tree, Margam Mountain, 2019

There's a public facility near my home, an urban outdoor space; a resource with a reservoir, a bird reserve, a path for walkers. Nature in those environments can feel uncomfortable at times—you have to ignore certain features, keep looking away.

Walking along the footpath one day, I find a black holdall by the side of the water. It seems displaced in such an ugly way. Someone else's things have been gone through, violated.

There are multiple openings—a black towel, ripped plastic sheeting, and the broken zipper of the holdall itself all pulled apart to reveal the beautiful fur of a dog, absolutely still. A body completely engulfed by bag, wrong in so many ways.

I touch it gently with my foot, feel its weight.

I take a picture, not knowing what else to do.

As well as photographs of the house, the archive holds many photographs taken on the beach at Caswell Bay; Thereza by the waterline, and others of her sitting on the rocks, in a different kind of pose, one that struck me as conspicuous.

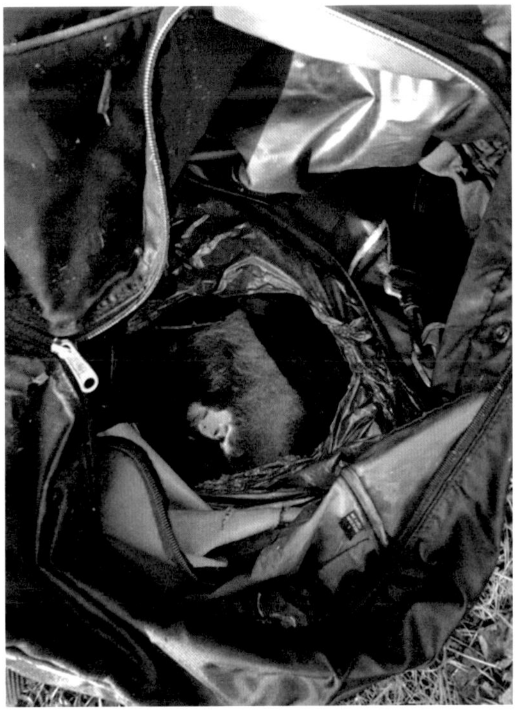

Dead Dog, Woodberry Down, 2017

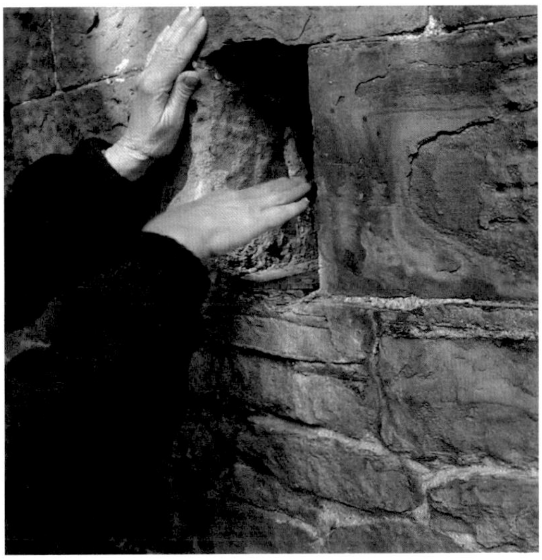

Demonstration, Observatory, Penllergare, 2018

An envelope marked 'photographs' comes home from my daughter's nursery one day, when she is about three. The picture inside shows her sitting in a rocking chair, in-expertly lit in an improvised studio: makeshift, provisional, immediately recognisable.

Her little hands are clamped together, one above the other and together they grip the arm of the chair, un-comprehending of the photographer's instructions, subjugated into obedient conformity through the act having her picture taken.

'What are you doing in that photograph?'

'Having my picture taken.'

I had an uneasy relationship with my daughter's keyworker, the intimacy between us, something between neediness and distrust, the slippage between service provider and service user.

I didn't know how to negotiate our relationship, how to navigate the terrain between accountability, tokenism and love.

Our dialogue was mediated through the operational procedures of Camden Council Early Years Trust. They functioned as a kind of buffer, moderating expectations, neurosis, tone.

My daughter's development was recorded on slips of paper by a variety of different hands, while I was at work, and she was left on an unfamiliar carpet, with scratched up CDs, chewed pens, dried pasta as playthings—some familiar from my own childhood nursery, the dimness of memory.

'Edie put a plastic tube on her arm, then she couldn't take it out. She came to me and showed her arm, saying "oh-oh"'

And somewhere deep down, a return, an echo, a nightmare.

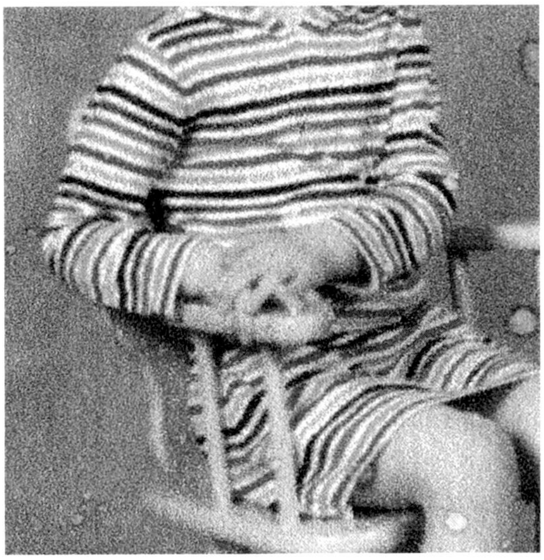

Young Girl, 2017/2017

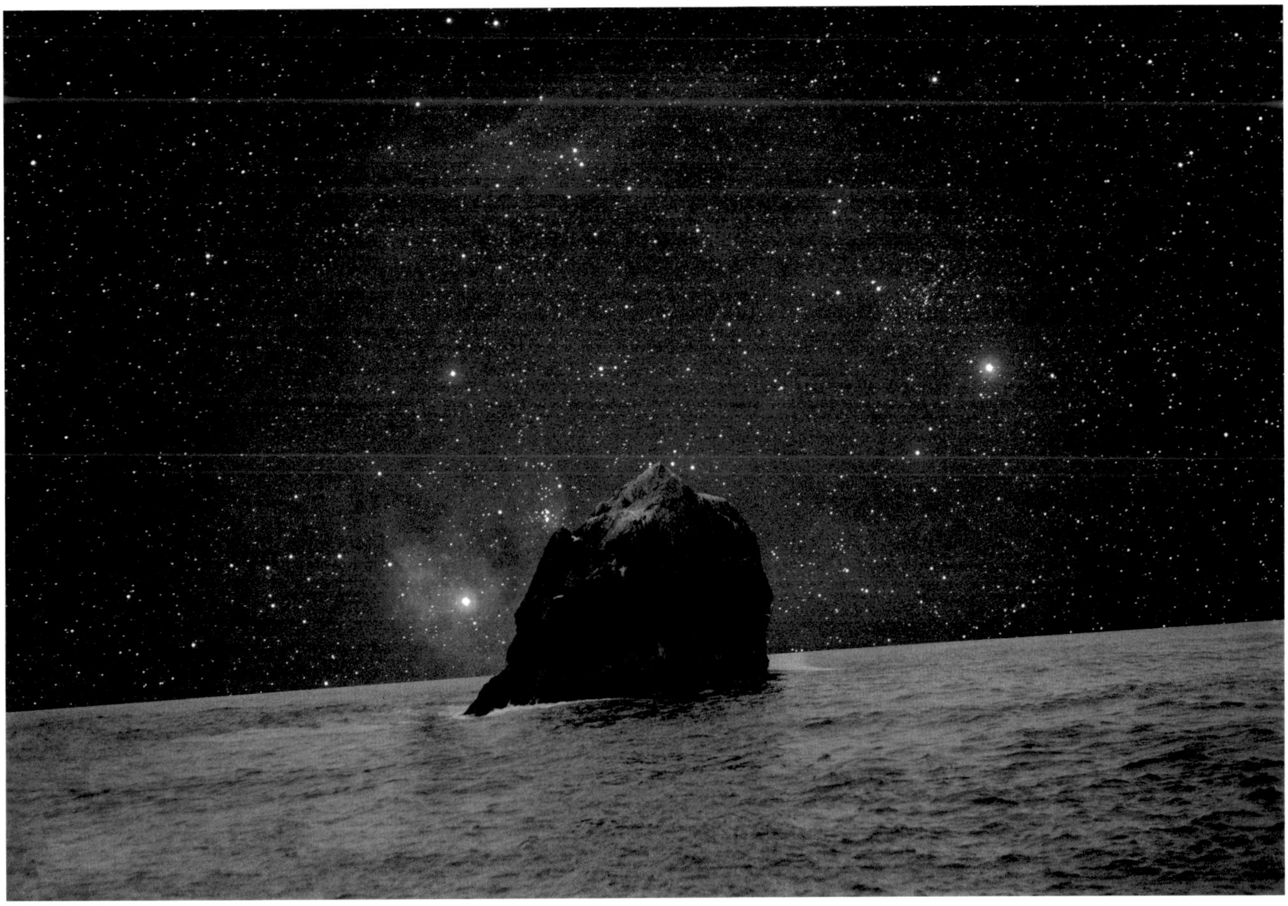

Rockall, 1961/2019

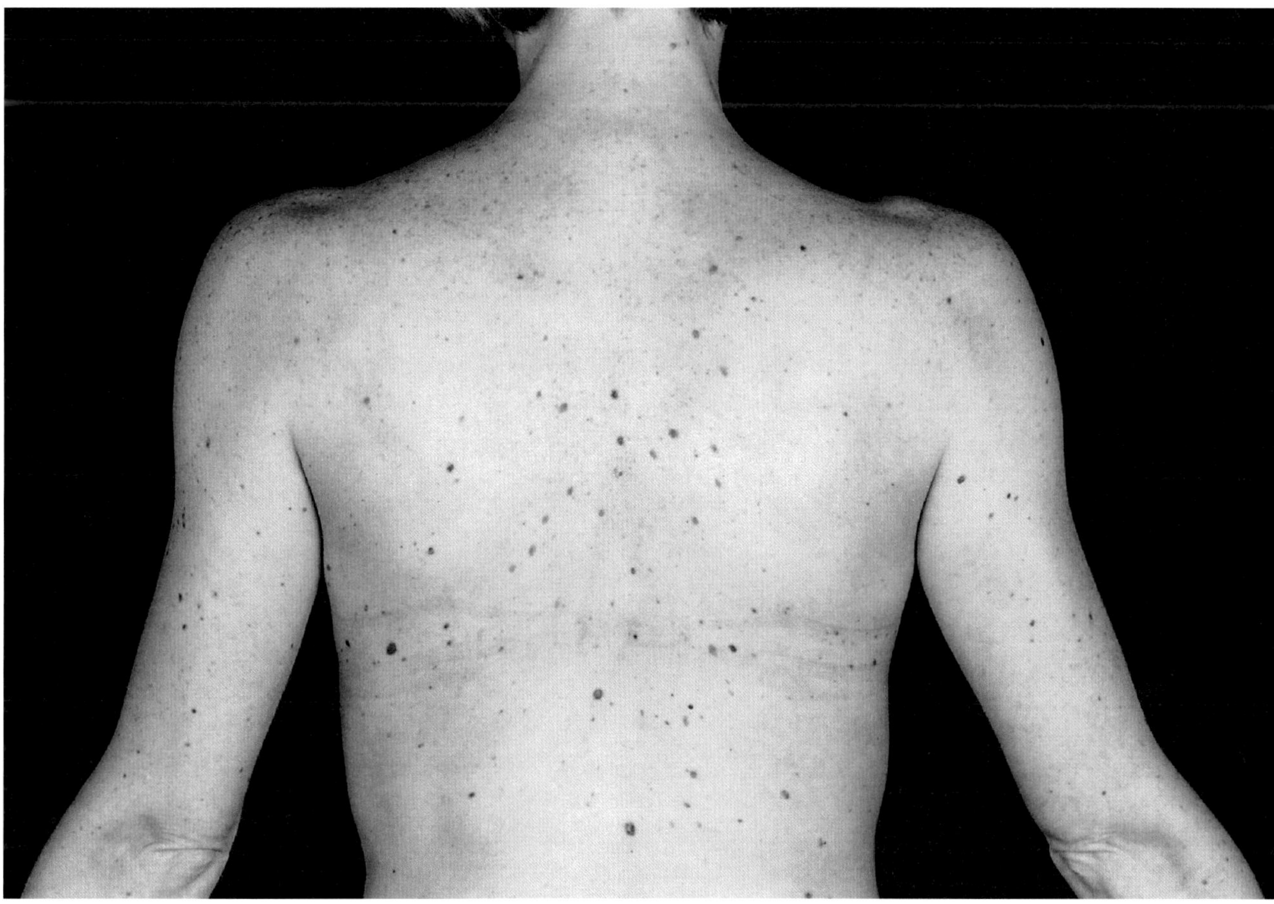

Young Woman/Observation (4), 1998/2019

Following spread
Escapes, Caswell Bay, 2017

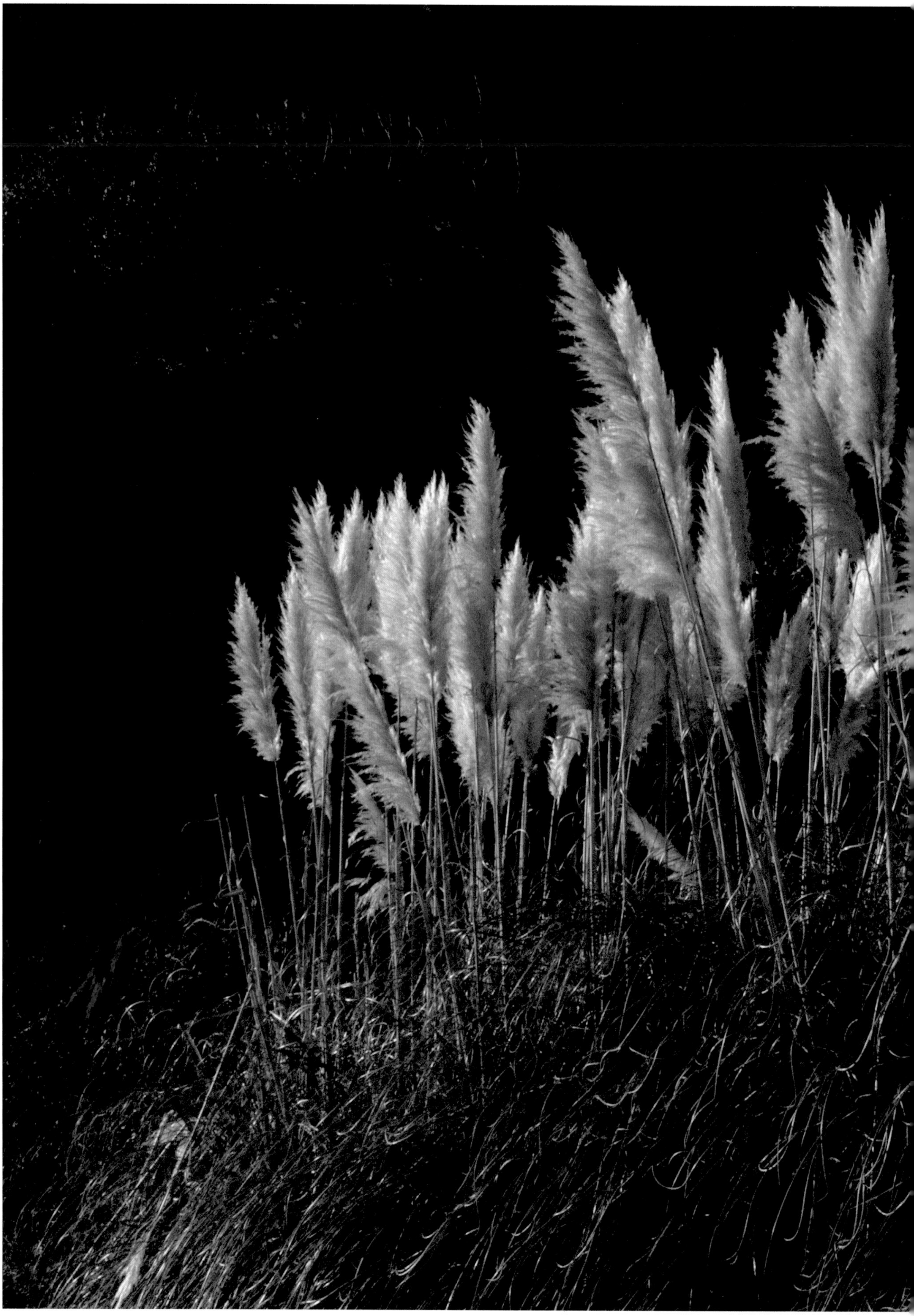

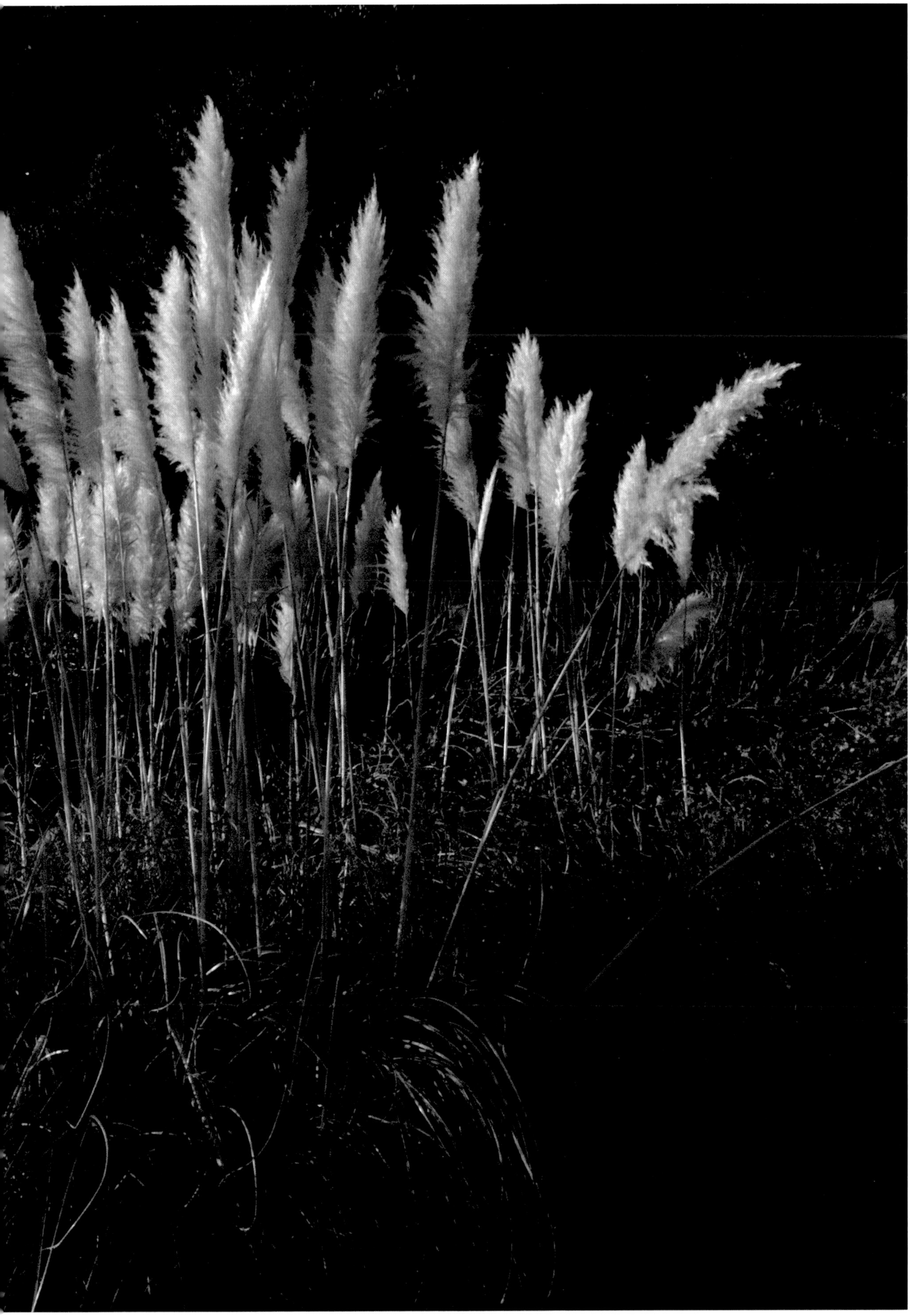

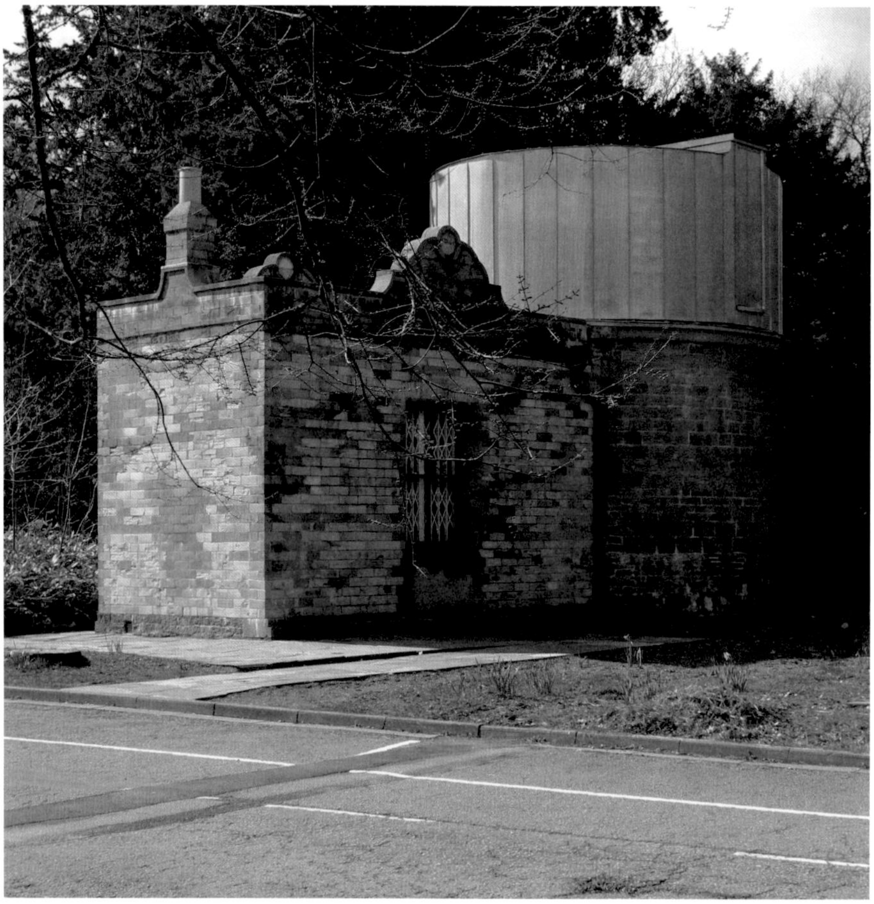

Observatory, Penllergare Valley Woods, 2018

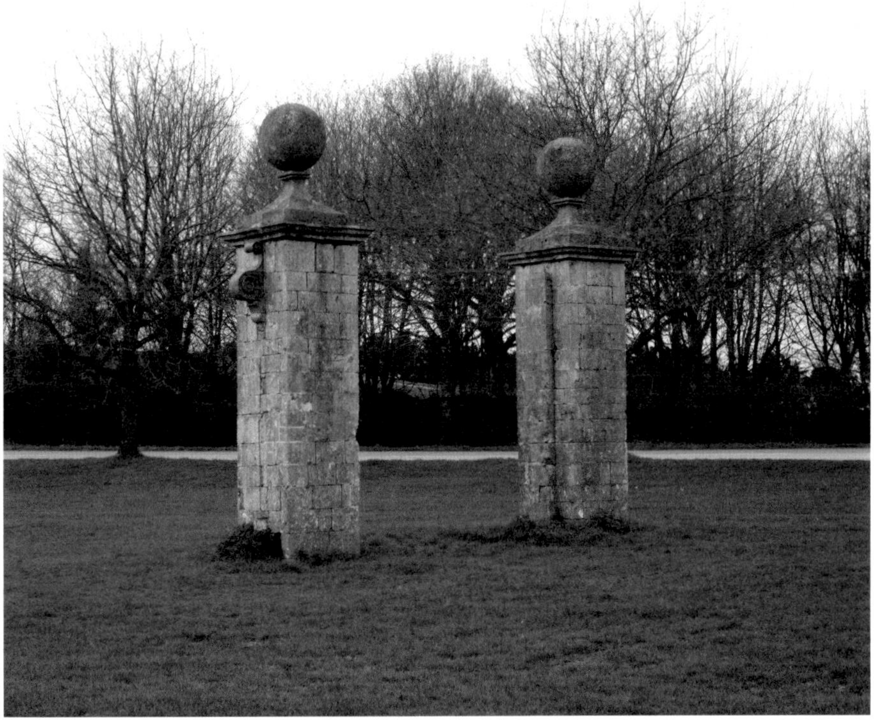

Gate Posts, former entrance to Margam Castle, Margam Country Park, 2019

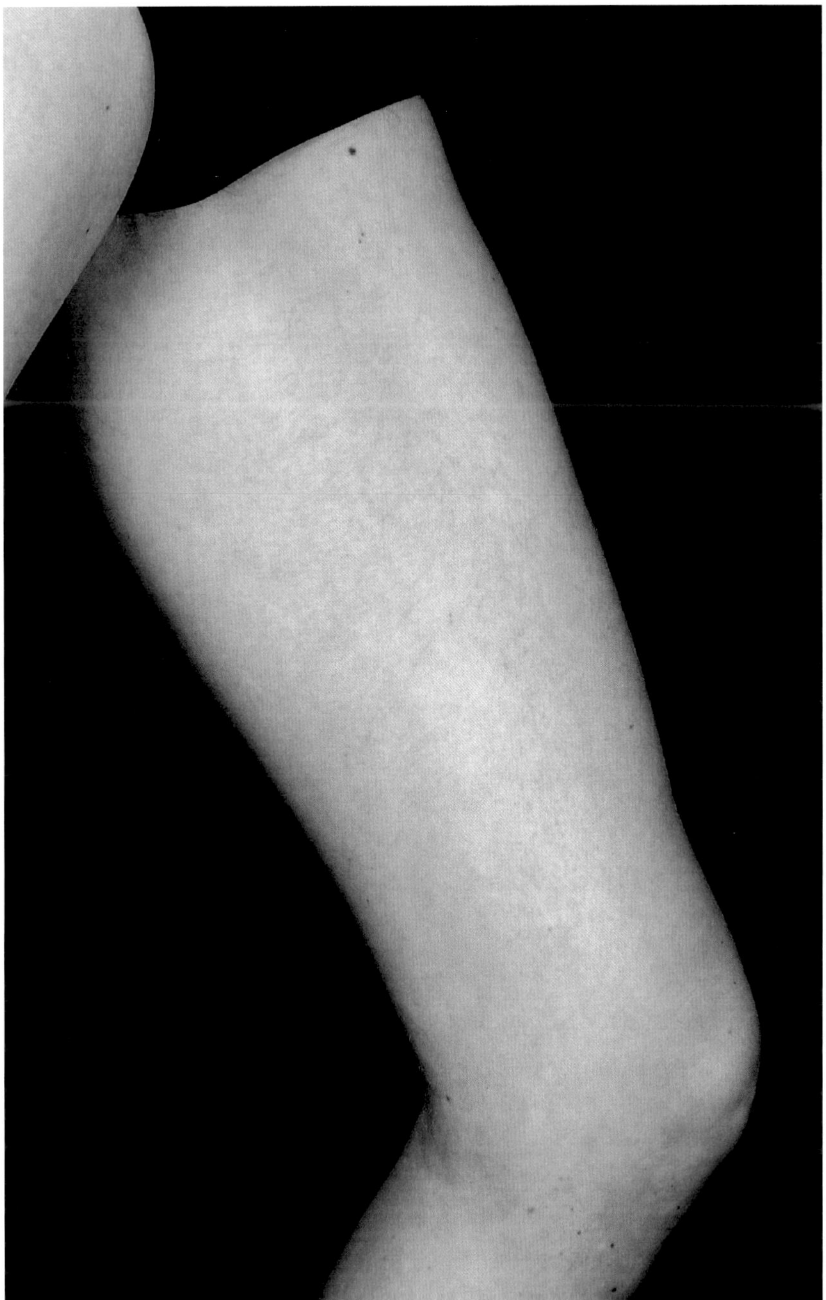

Young Woman/Observation (5), 1998/2019

The idea of the house at Caswell being under the carpark stays with me, the sense of it as still there, like the bones of Richard III; a layer in the statigraphic column, haunted.

I wonder if she will see me again, if she can be persuaded to be involved in the project after all, maybe just her hands.

Walking along the river the last time I see her, we talk about the erosion of the riverbank, about how the river still bends and folds in much the same way that it would have done in Thereza's time, its ebbs and flows subjecting the bank to the kind of forces of erosion that cause collapses, silting, small changes in its flow.

'It's doing what rivers do' she says. I like her manner, her briskness, her knowledge, her understanding.

Near the end of the walk, I ask if we might meet again, just one more time.

'Yes...'

She looks at me straight.

'But I think you have it all.'

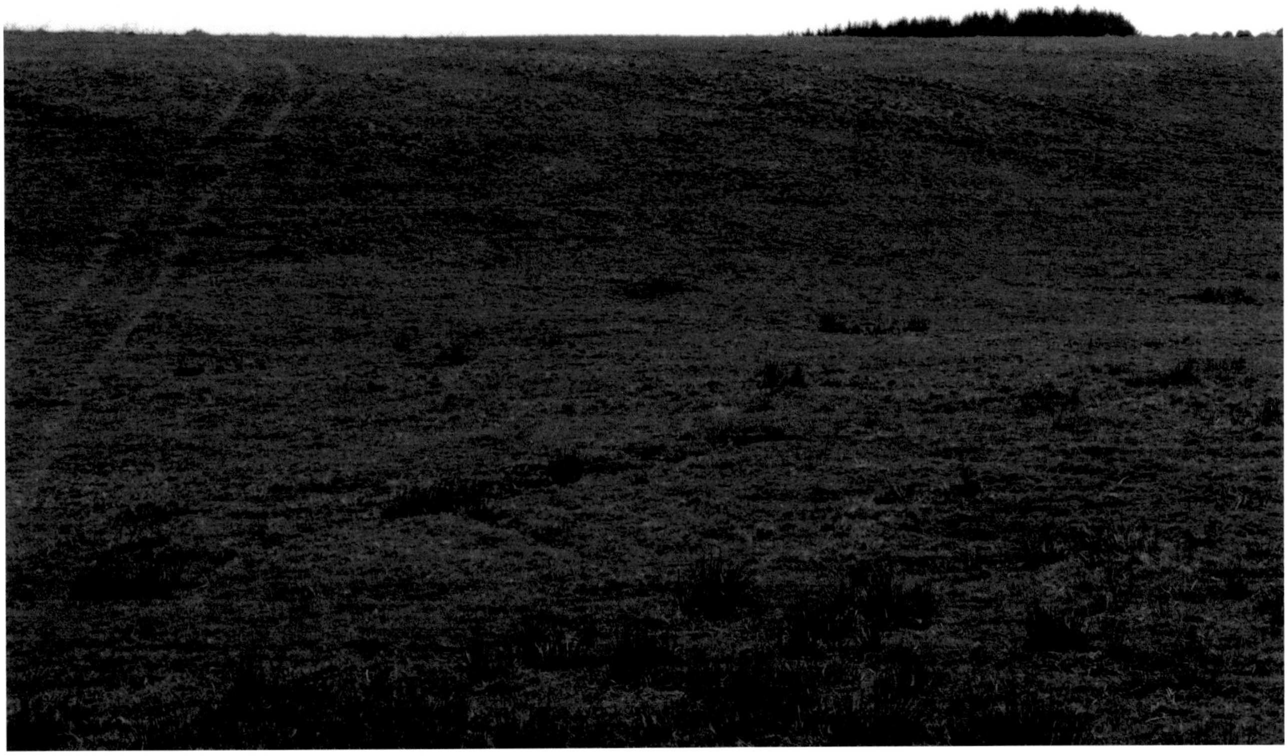

Foreshortened Hill, Margam Country Park, 2018

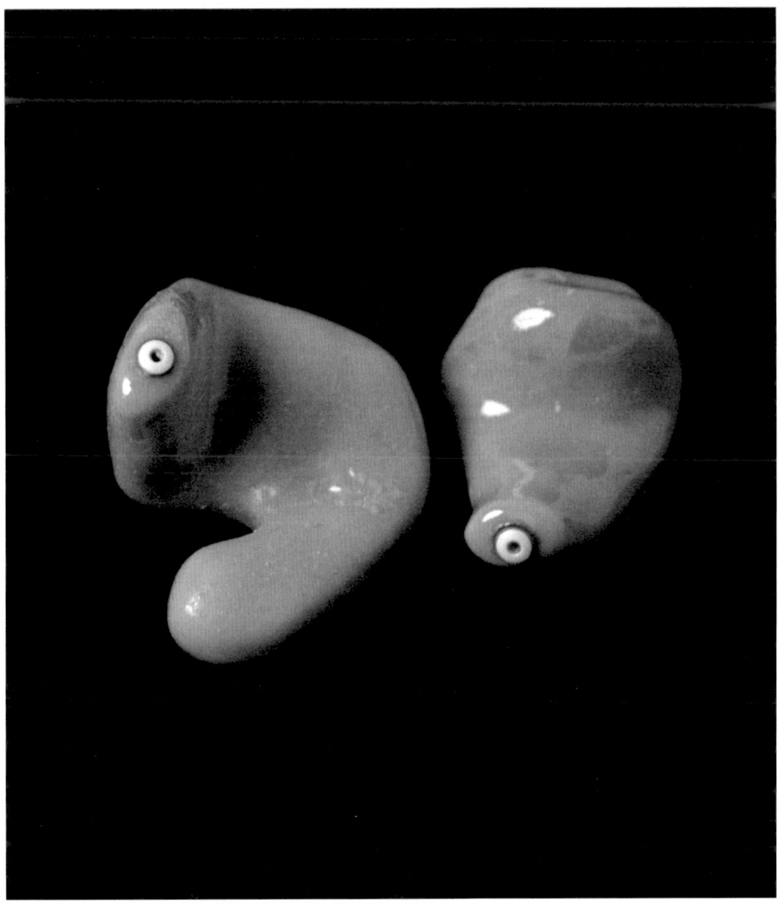

Hearing Aids, 2019

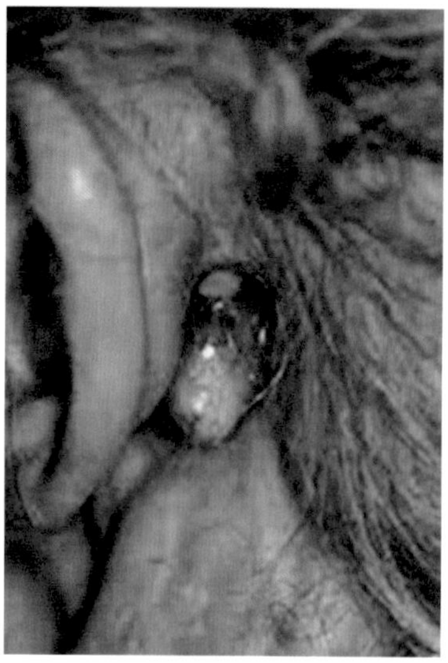

Mastoid/Observation, 2017/2019

Sophy Rickett
in conversation with
David Campany

David At what point did this project become a project? Was it clear from quite early? Or did there come a moment when you saw there was really something, beyond research, that was in it for you as an artist?

Sophy Things started falling into place while I was talking with Jennie, the trustee at Penllergare who introduced me to Thereza, and the Penllergare Valley Woods. The first time we met, Jennie and I talked for several hours. I enjoyed her presence, the way she expressed things, how she moved. I decided I would ask her to be a part of the project, maybe even to perform the role of guide to the camera. Then as we said goodbye, almost by chance, she said that she would be happy to meet again, and talk some more, but that she was not prepared to appear in the project, or to be featured in any way. I responded 'oh of course, that's fine, no problem,' but inside I felt stung and rejected, that I had been found out. But also I think that was the moment where I felt like I was on to something. Something about her refusal felt important. It was so adamant, with a resistance to me that generated a certain kind of energy, a determination to find and then explore a subject without ever bringing it fully into view.

I like that about photography—its failure to fully capture the subject. One of my favourite outtakes from the project is a Google Earth picture that shows the carpark in Leicester, where Richard III's remains were discovered. It must have been taken as part of a routine data capture, one of many millions of images, inconsequential at the time of its making, which became significant retrospectively. I like how the red circle that indicates the position of the remains is on the surface of the image, not in the pictorial space. I kept a copy of it, with the intention of including it somehow, because I mention it in the text, in relation to layers in the stratigraphic column; a reference to the idea that layers of time are held physically, forensically, in the earth.

David Yes, it seems that as a culture we've gone from belief in the truth-telling capacity of photography to a faith in the idea that despite itself, despite its inscrutability, despite its evasions and displacements, it cannot avoid being a clue to... something. Perhaps something unconscious or unintended. It might be hiding in plain sight, or buried, or just beyond what's captured. We're not able to just walk away from photography as if it had been debunked and called out. I suspect it is often precisely the inscrutability that prompts our desire to know the secrets of the image. (I feel like we're back with William Henry Fox Talbot's assertion that if photography is evidence, it is 'evidence of novel kind'). Of course, all this puts the photograph in a strange relation to art, as something to look at and look through, or beyond. A thing in itself and an unpredictable, winding path to something else. Does this ring true to you?

Sophy The project became like an investigation—but one that went awry, because I didn't know exactly what I was looking for, just that I had an urge to look for, to record, as you say, something.

I started using photography in a very literal way if that makes sense; snapping my way through, gathering visual data that I suspected would be unhelpful in that it would reveal very little about the subject. And in the end, it was that leaning into the process of photography that became interesting. So I wasn't really thinking about truth or realism, I was thinking more about rhetoric, and how photography can be made to fail, and yet still to seduce.

David Ha, yes. Failure has its seductions, and seduction is bound to fail. There's often a strange conundrum when one first approaches an archive in an open-ended way. The archivist asks (or we ask of ourselves): 'What are you looking for?' 'Umm, what do you have?' 'Well, it depends what you're looking for. I can't show you everything.' In a way I think that making photographs is a bit like this. One knows there is an image to be taken, but it's not clear how or why, or what it should be. One is waiting for something to reveal itself as having possibility. And perhaps looking at photographs is like this too. We look with intent but we often don't know what we are intending or what we want. It can all feel like fumbling around until something happens.

Sophy So much dogma builds up around heritage and art historical contexts, well maybe it does around everything (including photography, and its written history), so yes, I agree, it feels important to stay open to the affective dimension of even the driest situation. I like the process of finding my own angle, looking askance, muscling my way in.

This time, as I circled around the subject—the archives, the places Thereza mentions in her diaries—certain points were made repeatedly. None of them were neutral—they all seemed to come from an ideological position; new housing developments spoil the countryside, the presence of the M4 motorway has no place in the otherwise picturesque tranquillity of Penllergare, and so on. I became interested in creating my own access points to the history, ones where misunderstanding, disagreement and chance were as productive and meaningful as the officially accepted version of events. I let myself be distracted, meander through, using photography to notionally record my journey, but also at the same time, knowing I was getting it 'wrong.'

One idea I had was to conduct detailed research into the construction of the M4, in relation to the concrete; where it had come from, and how it was constituted materially. I also wrote about the drainage pipes that ran under the motorway, directing the River Llan, a trickle that far from the sea, into the Penllergare estate. It made me think of the concave wave breaks on the beach in Teignmouth, near where I grew up, and for a while I thought about writing about when I was a kid and trying to get into a comfortable position but my body never really fitted.

David I often find myself in a similar position in relation to archival research. Archives are sites not of meaning but of potential meaning, and it always depends who is doing the asking and what they think they want. But we often feel there's some kind of hidden truth to an archive, if only we could grasp it, or make the 'correct' approach. In other words, it's as if the archive wants to throw our own ignorance in our faces. I wonder if it is this that leads us to make our approaches playful rather than dutiful, emancipated rather than trapped.

Sophy Even if I think I have found a way in to an archive that's different to any I have taken in the past, I'll often then find that I have been circling and revisiting the same themes. There can be something reassuring about that; the sense of a negotiation between me and the world that is ongoing, unresolved. It's not so much about having an interest or concern that motivates me; it's more like having a preoccupation—something sticky that puts me to work. I choose a direction, but I also feel pulled.

This project took longer than most to settle, it kept pulling in different directions. And at some point that seemed right as well; its resistance to closure.

David I'm interested in what you say about the persistence of certain preoccupations, and that the finding of, or stumbling into projects has something to do with finding an outlet for them. That's different from a photographer who is interested in a specific kind of subject matter, for example. Your subject matter has varied greatly over the years and yet, as you say, the preoccupations have remained consistent. I guess at a certain point one looks back and can see that despite the variety, one's work does have consistency, even a fateful consistency. However far one wanders, something in the method reveals itself. Is there something about photography that permits this for you?

Sophy Thinking about it now, photography is a preoccupation that has sustained my interest for many years—not as a process, but as a theme, a subject in itself. I experience strong resistances to it; it can feel so claustrophobic, its emphasis on subject. But there's something about photography that works for me; its slipperiness, its plasticity. I think I can be impatient and restless, a little bit jumpy, and that's consistent with my understanding of photography, and also something I like about it; its fragmented, non-chronological-ness, its flattening out, and the way the subject of a photograph is so often outside of the frame.

David This raises interesting questions, or challenges about how a project resolves. Not simply how it takes shape, but the moment where some kind of closure, however provisional it is, seems possible. I get the impression that very often artists engagements with archives end provisionally, not quite with abandonment but with a feeling that no clear ending is possible, concluding that maybe there is nothing to conclude. The meaning of the work lies in something other than resolution.

Sophy My story begins and ends with Jennie at Penllergare who said when we first met that she was not prepared to be featured in my work, or to appear in it in any way.

The ending as I came to understand it happened around the fourth or fifth occasion we met, by which time I'd begun to feel I was badgering her, circling around the topic, asking questions in the hope that something other than what I had thought to ask would be revealed.

So we were walking along the River Lan one afternoon and she was in front. I was trying to figure out how to convince her to appear in the film and was only half listening when she began to say how the bends and folds in the river would have been much the same in Thereza's time as they are now; a similar structure, with a slightly differentconfiguration. She talked about the compression of the mud, and how it would break off intermittently in heavy clods and the silt would build up and the flow of water would, over time, gently alter.

It was an expression of continuity that seemed to capture how I'd been thinking, and I decided to ask her whether we could meet up again, to talk about that further. And then we were standing still, on the compressed mud, the river brook at our feet, and she looked at me and said, 'Sophy, I think you have it all,' and I felt myself being gently admonished.

'I think you have it all.' It is such a strong phrase; an affirmation, but also on some level, a rebuke. It opened something out for me, the sense of already having everything I needed and the work I had to do was figuring out how to make it make sense. And at the same time, there was something in her look that said she wanted to close down, that she was asking me to stop. 'Sophy, you have it all.' She didn't mean it like that but on some level it landed, and in that moment I felt a little bit ashamed.

David I have the feeling that people are often like the institutions they work for, or run. They have some of the same qualities. That's inevitable, I imagine, because people feel some kind of affinity with the institution to even decide to work for it, and then people grow into their jobs, become them. Not completely, but substantially. This relationship between institutions and their people seems more emphatic and indivisible to an outsider. Plus of course the objects in an institution like an archive also seem to take on the same qualities as the institution and its people. Welcoming, but never quite able to give you what you want, or even help you figure out what you want, because you don't know quite what you want until you find it. So everything surrounding one's open curiosity can feel unsubstantiated. 'You have it all'—maybe not the words, but the way a searching person receives them—is bound to feel like a foreclosure. And it's something photographs 'say' to us all the time. 'Here you are. This is all I have to offer. It should be enough for you. If it isn't... I don't know what more I can do.'

Sophy Yes, as if it cannot hold the subject down very firmly... The last picture I took for *The Curious Moaning of Kenfig Burrows*, was of a pair of hearing aids. I wasn't expecting a picture of hearing aids themselves to say anything much about hearing loss, but what I was interested in was the hearing aid's very strange visual presence. The ones I bought on eBay look like embryos, with little staring eyes created by the audio output transmitter. They fit perfectly, into the ear canal, and transmit sound deep into the brain. I found something in those unseeing eyes, something mechanical and cold, yet also weirdly sentient. Humanoid boneless structures with eyes but no mouth, silent and a little bit scary. Mute, indestructible. And on some level that reminds me of the condition of hearing loss; the distance, the isolation, the sense of something completely unknown. Photography performs what we bring to it.

For the female subjects
who inspired and guided this book;
my daughter, my sister, my mum,
Jennie, Lily May
and, of course, Thereza

The Curious Moaning of Kenfig Burrows was originally commissioned by Glynn Vivian Gallery, Swansea in 2016, to form part of the exhibition *The Moon and a Smile*, from an idea developed by Helen Sear, Katy Freer and Jenni Spencer-Davies.

The artist would like to thank everyone at GOST especially Stu Smith who edited and designed this book, and Claudia, Katie and Gemma; Anouchka Grose; Bettina von Zwehl; David Campany; Mark Etheridge at National Museum Wales; Jennie Eyres; the team at Metro Imaging, especially Sean for his beautiful printing and Simon, Steve, Rhiannon, Ciaran, Tony, Andy, David, and Tom at Brider and Bull.

Thanks also to the research department at UAL: London College of Communication for their ongoing assistance and financial support.

The Curious Moaning of Kenfig Burrows
First published in 2019 by
GOST Books
8a West Smithfield
London
ec1a 9jr
info@gostbooks.com
gostbooks.com

Designed and produced by GOST:
Katie Clifford, Gemma Gerhard, Justine Hucker, Allon Kaye, Eleanor Macnair, Claudia Paladini, Ana Rocha

Printed in Italy by EBS

British Library cataloguing-in-publication data. A catalogue record of this book is available from the British Library.

isbn 978-1-910401-30-9